The **21**

The 21

A Journey into the Land of Coptic Martyrs

Martin Mosebach

Translated by Alta L. Price

PLOUGH PUBLISHING HOUSE

Published by Plough Publishing House
Walden, New York
Robertsbridge, England
Elsmore, Australia
www.plough.com

Plough produces books, a quarterly magazine, and Plough.com to encourage people and help them put their faith into action. We believe Jesus can transform the world and that his teachings and example apply to all aspects of life. At the same time, we seek common ground with all people regardless of their creed.

Plough is the publishing house of the Bruderhof, an international community of families and singles seeking to follow Jesus together. Members of the Bruderhof are committed to a way of radical discipleship in the spirit of the Sermon on the Mount. Inspired by the first church in Jerusalem (Acts 2 and 4), they renounce private property and share everything in common in a life of nonviolence, justice, and service to neighbors near and far. To learn more about the Bruderhof's faith, history, and daily life, see Bruderhof.com. (Views expressed by Plough authors are their own and do not necessarily reflect the position of the Bruderhof.)

ISBN: 978-0-87486-839-5
23 22 21 20 19   1 2 3 4 5 6 7 8

Originally published under the title *Die 21: Eine Reise ins Land der Koptischen Martyrer.* Copyright © 2018 by Rowohlt Verlag GmbH, Reinbek bei Hamburg, Germany. English translation copyright © 2019 by Alta L. Price. The translation of this work was supported by a grant from the Goethe-Institut.

A catalog record for this book is available from the British Library.
Library of Congress Cataloging-in-Publication Data

Names: Mosebach, Martin, 1951- author. | Price, Alta L., translator.
Title: The 21 : a journey into the land of Coptic martyrs / Martin Mosebach ;
    translated by Alta L. Price.
Other titles: 21. English | Twenty-one
Description: Walden, New York : Published by Plough Publishing House, 2018. |
    "Originally published under the title Die 21: Eine Reise ins Land der
    Koptischen Martyrer. Copyright 2018 by Rowohlt Verlag GmbH, Reinbek bei
    Hamburg, Germany. English translation copyright 2018 by Alta L. Price.
    The translation of this work was supported by a grant from the
    Goethe-Institut."
Identifiers: LCCN 2018045618 (print) | LCCN 2018047401 (ebook) | ISBN
    9780874868401 (epub) | ISBN 9780874868418 (mobi) | ISBN 9780874868425 (
    pdf) | ISBN 9780874868395 (hardcover)
Subjects: LCSH: Mosebach, Martin, 1951---Travel--Egypt. |
    Copts--Egypt--Social conditions--21st century. | Copts--Egypt--Religious
    life and customs. | Martyrs--Egypt--Biography. | Coptic Christian
    saints--Egypt--Biography.
Classification: LCC DT72.C7 (ebook) | LCC DT72.C7 M6713 2018 (print) | DDC
    962.004932--dc23
LC record available at https://lccn.loc.gov/2018045618

Printed in the United States of America

The Twenty-One Copts

Martyred on February 15, 2015

Tawadros Youssef Tawadros, born September 16, 1968, in El-Aour, Samalut

Magued Seliman Shehata, born August 24, 1973, in El-Aour, Samalut

Hany Abd el Messiah, born January 1, 1982, in El-Aour, Samalut

Ezzat Boushra Youssef, born August 14, 1982, in Dafash, Samalut

Malak (the elder) Farag Ibrahim, born January 1, 1984, in Al-Subi, Samalut

Samuel (the elder) Alham Wilson, born July 14, 1986, in El-Aour, Samalut

Malak (the younger) Ibrahim Seniut, born September 9, 1986, in El-Aour, Samalut

Luka Nagati Anis, born in January, 1987, in Mashat Manqatin, Samalut

Sameh Salah Farouk, born May 20, 1988, in Menqarios, Samalut

Milad Makin Zaky, born October 1, 1988, in El-Aour, Samalut

Issam Baddar Samir, born April 15, 1990, in El-Helmeya

Youssef Shoukry Younan, born June 2, 1990, in El-Aour, Samalut

Bishoy Stefanos Kamel, born September 4, 1990, in El-Aour, Samalut

Abanub Ayat Shahata, born July 22, 1991, in El-Aour, Samalut

Girgis (the elder) Samir Megally, born October 1, 1991, in Samsum, Samalut

Mina Fayez Aziz, born October 8, 1991, in El-Aour, Samalut

Kiryollos Boushra Fawzy, born November 11, 1991, in El-Aour, Samalut

Gaber Mounir Adly, born January 25, 1992, in Menbal, Matay

Samuel (the younger) Stefanos Kamel, born November 26, 1992, in El-Aour, Samalut

Girgis (the younger) Milad Seniut, born December 17, 1992, in El-Aour, Samalut

Matthew Ayariga, from Ghana

A note on names: Egyptians do not generally have last names as traditionally formulated in most Western countries. Instead, their name is composed of a given name followed by the given names of their father and grandfather. Egyptians known internationally often use their father's given name as a Western last name.

Contents

Kiryollos

1

The Head of Saint Kiryollos

THE PICTURE ON THE COVER of a magazine drew me in: it showed the head of a young man, evidently of Mediterranean origin, surrounded by a bit of orange-colored fabric. He was a lean youth with brownish skin, a sharp hairline, and a rather light mustache, his eyes half closed; his thin lips were slightly parted, offering a glimpse of his teeth. His expression wasn't exactly a smile – it was more one of deep relaxation, such that his mouth had involuntarily opened to take in a deep breath or let out a sigh.

Only later did I learn that the photo had been cropped, and that I had been misled. I hadn't initially gathered that this head had been severed from its body. In fact, there were no signs that this man had suffered any violence. If his face had tensed during the decapitation, or if pain or fear had made themselves visible, then any sign of these things had vanished the instant he died.

The image showed the moment immediately after the crime. It came from a video taken by his killers to document their deeds and spread terror worldwide. Strangely, though, separated from its broader context, it didn't inspire fear, at least not at first. This was not yet the head of a dead man. After the beheading, a flicker of consciousness and warmth had lingered a moment on his face – an eternal moment of dreaming and slumber, in which the finality of what had just happened no longer seemed important. The cruel and sudden severing of this life had already created a new condition: all else receded into the past. And yet, at the moment captured in the picture, the sum total of his existence – about to recede for good but still present in his head – was somehow tangible one last time.

I have since learned his name: Kiryollos Boushra Fawzy, born November 11, 1991, in the Upper Egyptian village of El-Aour in the diocese of Samalut. His patron saint was Cyril of Alexandria, who at the fifth-century Council of Ephesus played a significant part in establishing the title of *Theotokos*, "Mother of God," for Jesus' mother. Unlike Cyril of Alexandria, though, Kiryollos did not play even a modest role in Egyptian public life when he was alive. He was one of far too many who cannot find work in their own country. That did not prevent him from becoming one of the saints of the Coptic Orthodox Church, however, just like his namesake. Only two weeks after the massacre, Tawadros II of Alexandria, Pope of the Coptic Orthodox Church, added Kiryollos's name to the *Synaxarium*, the liturgical list of Coptic martyrs; his image is now worshiped on icons.

In the February 15, 2015, video showing his execution – and that of his twenty companions – I see him alive. He kneels in an upright position before his executioner. He looks relaxed; his curiously indifferent gaze seemingly directed at the beach in front of him, as though he wanted to take in every last detail. Since then I have also found a passport photo of him, likely from 2009. He was a soldier at the time, and his black felt beret features the insignia of the Egyptian Republic: an eagle centered on a black, white, and red flag. The image shows that he had a palsy – his left eyelid is drooped, partially obscuring his eye – although it clearly did not prevent him from passing the medical exam. In this picture, too, a sliver of his teeth can be seen, although his lips are closed.

Christianity's history is rife with beheadings. The severed head of John the Baptist, Jesus' forerunner, is the subject of numerous paintings and mosaics, several of which have become widely appreciated works of art. John the Baptist was beheaded before Jesus was crucified, to satisfy the whim of an enraged queen. Then came Paul the Apostle, who, as a Roman citizen, was granted the privilege of requesting death by decapitation, thereby sparing himself the fate of being tortured to death – a punishment reserved for slaves. From then on, countless heads have rolled for maintaining their belief in Jesus Christ, even in predominantly Christian countries: consider the case of Sir Thomas More under King Henry VIII in England, or Alexander Schmorell, a member of the White Rose in Nazi Germany, who was later canonized by the Russian Orthodox Church Outside of Russia.

And yet such figures feel far removed from us, as if they belong to some other, seemingly incomprehensible era. Much as the brutal nature of their deaths and the firmness, even stubbornness, with which they confessed their faith seem to match one another in context, we find their fate equally eerie. Hasn't the Western world, with its openness toward discussion and dialogue, long since overcome the need for opposites to be regarded as life-threatening? We live in an era of strict religious privatization, and want to see it subjected to secular law. Society seems to have reached a consensus on the rejection of proselytizing and religious zeal. Hasn't all that put an end to the merciless, all-or-nothing alternatives of believe or leave; or worse, renounce your faith or die?

But the photo of Kiryollos's severed head, and the video showing his companions' severed heads, are only a few years old. What does this apparent anachronism mean? Should we read it as a sign that our idea of historical progress was mere delusion? That martyrdom and Christianity go hand in hand through every historical era, and that as long as there are Christians there will also be martyrs?

The head on the cover of the magazine would not let me go. Many readers were outraged, as an editor who had also been disturbed told me when I asked about it. But I wanted to keep it with me – I saved the clipping, and frequently contemplated it at length.

Kiryollos was the first of the fallen to step forward out of anonymity for me. The twenty-one men beheaded on the beach near the port town of Sirte, Libya, are always regarded as a group, just like the young martyrs of the Theban Legion, who were also from Egypt. Only one of the group was not a Copt, and came, as has since been learned, from Ghana, in West Africa. But because the Copts have considered him one of their own since his death, I, too, choose to refer to them here as the "Twenty-One."

The Coptic community and its Christian traditions, which have been faithfully preserved since the early apostolic age, are not well known in the West. The Roman Catholic Church has long cultivated a certain arrogance with regard to Eastern Christians, who are not in communion with Rome, and that fact prevents many, especially Catholics, from looking eastward. Not long after the Twenty-One were beheaded, I met with a German cardinal. I asked him why the Catholic Church did not formally recognize the testimony of these men of faith, as the old church generally had in cases of martyrdom. "But they're Copts!" he answered. I will not mention this high church dignitary by name, because I do not believe his helpless words should be heard as an expression of his own personal views. Wasn't he simply saying precisely what many of his peers would have, if given the chance? Right then and there I decided that I had to learn more about the Copts, and the Twenty-One in particular.

How might I get closer to them and find out more about their lives, their origins, and the circumstances in which they grew up? There are so many historic martyrs we know so little about, other than a few inaccurate details of their deaths; the dry lists of the *Martyrologium Romanum*, the Catholic Church's official register of saints, remained abstract until Christian art turned them into tangible, relatable images. Things are rather different with the Twenty-One: not only is there a video of their Passion, but this video has the selfsame intention and effect as a work of art, albeit a particularly vile one – it is at once both document and aesthetically staged, pathetic concoction. Stretching our definition of "art" to such a degree may seem inappropriate, but mustn't we admit that the video is effective, carefully choreographed, and designed with an attentive eye for color? Aren't there other realms where the border between art and reality has become dangerously blurred? For many, the increasing surrealness of the world has aroused a hunger for absolute authenticity. And isn't it an enhancement to the spectacle when the blood bathing the stage is real?

The Twenty-One could well have echoed the words of Paul the Apostle: "For we are made a spectacle unto the world, and to angels, and to men." But before they became such a spectacle for God and the world, each led the unremarkable life of a poor farmer. Seen in retrospect, this could be considered nothing more than apt preparation for their martyrdom. So was there anything in their villages that might have foreshadowed all this? In February and March of 2017, two years after the massacre, I traveled to Upper Egypt, to the homes they had left when they set out for Libya in search of work.

الشهيد/ صموئيل الهم

يا ربى يسوع

Samuel (the elder)

2

What I Tell and What I Do Not Tell

THE TWENTY-ONE COPTIC MIGRANT WORKERS were beheaded on a Libyan beach after the killers' leader called upon "merciful Allah"; the video documenting the murder describes itself as "Muhammad's answer" to the "nation of the cross." The language is clear – the situation seems to need no further explanation. Two equal sides are in opposition, a murderer for every victim. This was evidently important to the event's choreographers: the idea that the sacred purification of the world must be carried out individually, by each pure soul. That such pure souls must necessarily dirty their own hands, that the death of nonbelievers is good, and that it is even better to kill nonbelievers oneself, with one's own hands – this is a task to be completed, a serious duty.

This is how I understand what this "message" to the "nation of the cross" intends to say, and yet I know just as little as anyone else about who was actually behind this crime. Masks hid the faces of the perpetrators, and even after some of them were arrested in October 2017, including the video's cameraman, their nations of origin are still unknown. They are members of the belligerent terrorist troops of the Islamic State – though in Egypt many devout, educated Muslims claim that a vast array of contradictory, inconsistent interests are hidden behind this frightening name, interests that have nothing to do with religion and everything to do with the influence world powers have on the Middle East. How, they rhetorically ask, could faithful, God-loving people commit murder?

One must be careful not to view this massacre as one more chapter of an ongoing religious war – that would be a false use of religion, invoking it solely to fuel the dispute in Egypt, justify the military dictatorship, and incite Western nations to intervene with weapons, air strikes, and troops. Just once, as we consider this crime, let's try posing the classic investigators' question: *Cui bono?* – Who benefits? The answers will likely constitute a garish bouquet of hypotheses in which the name of nearly every world power involved in the war in the Middle East pops up: Americans and Russians, dictators in Syria and Egypt, the hostile Muslim Brotherhood, Israel and the Gulf States, Iran and Turkey – somehow anything is plausible, since it's apparent that none of the forces involved in this "Islamic world's Thirty Years' War," as some commentators have dubbed it, is interested in putting an end to it. Did the killers act out of some deeply perverted zeal, or are they just unscrupulous mercenaries who can be bought to commit all kinds of bloodshed? Do they hold sole responsibility, as terrorists who've lost all sense of control, or are they just peons – pawns on a board whose actual players and goals are unknown even to them?

These questions have many answers – too many. They include expert opinions but also wild rumors, and sometimes both come to a similar conclusion. And can the perpetrators' portrayal of themselves, as shown in the notorious video, even be believed? Isn't it reckless to trust men capable of such acts?

I admit that I hadn't yet grappled with these questions when I made the decision to learn more about the decapitated Copts. I also had no intention, when I set off for Egypt, to learn anything more about the perpetrators. It was enough for me to leave them in the darkness they themselves aspired to. To call the political situation underlying the massacre on the Libyan beach *complicated* is a fussy euphemism. Anyone who has taken in even the most superficial bit of contradiction-laden news from this region of the world knows as much. Another question I wasn't seeking to answer was whether Islam, the religion of the Prophet Muhammad, contains in its purest form elements that fundamentally complicate Muslims' ability to live alongside believers of other religions – a hotly contested question nowadays. Here, then, Islam will only be mentioned when it touches upon Coptic lives.

I was significantly more moved by, and motivated to know more about, the fate of the murdered men for whom, I suspect, things had been rather simple. Some of them could read, but probably couldn't write, as there was no need to in their daily lives. They hadn't taken part in the political discussions frequent among Egyptian intellectuals – even the subject matter of such debates would probably have been incomprehensible to them, because their daily toil aimed to meet the kind of modest needs that, from loftier points of view, seem insignificant: providing for a wife, parents, and children; saving for a new house; buying seeds to sow in small fields; perhaps even putting some money aside, in case misfortune struck. These tasks shaped their daily lives much as it did the donkeys upon whose backs they unthinkingly strapped heavy loads, since they themselves were so used to bearing such burdens. Their gaze sunk in the field's furrows, unable to rise beyond their narrow horizons. People looking on from the viewpoint of Western civilization, as well as Cairo's academics, might well describe these men this way, and find ample material to back it up. Yet such a summation would be wrong, or at least grossly incomplete.

We have become accustomed to assuming that it is primarily political and economic motives that lie behind every religious conflict, because we don't want to consider the fact that a person's faith might actually be the ultimate, highest reality. But for these twenty-one Coptic peasants and migrant workers, that is precisely what their religion was. They lived in a world where, for the past several centuries, being Christian wasn't a given. For their long line of ancestors, belonging to Christianity had always meant being willing to bear witness to their faith. They were well aware of the disadvantages associated with being a Christian in Egypt. But these people who superficially seemed so weak, who eked out such a meager existence, were willing to accept these disadvantages. They didn't seem to struggle over the decision: what they held already, in the form of faith, was infinitely more precious to them than anything they could have acquired if they gave it up. Life itself, without faith, would have been worthless to them. It would be mere existence – an existence more lowly than that of the animals, for animals are perfect in and of themselves, but humans are imperfect; their aim for perfection requires divine assistance.

That is why I found it repugnant when the Twenty-One were referred to as "victims of terrorism." The word "victim" seemed too passive to me, implying an unwilling-ness – a giving in to something forced, something one might complain about. None of that, I thought, suited the Twenty-One. I suspected they had a strength that granted them a well-protected inner core of independence, and I was convinced their murderers' cruelty couldn't penetrate that deep.

The fate of Coptic Christians in Egypt does not look bright, and it doesn't take an oracle to predict rough times ahead. But we mustn't forget that the Copts have fared badly or very badly ever since the Islamic conquest of the country in the seventh century, meaning that they have had it hard for the last fourteen hundred years or so. Our present day marks just one more instance in a long series of scourges. The Twenty-One in Libya certainly weren't the first Copts ever killed – the list of prior crimes is long – and what has followed seems to be an attempt to surpass all previous horrors. The blood on the walls of Cairo's St. Peter and St. Paul Church, where just before Christmas 2016 twenty-four women and the sexton were shot during prayers, had not yet dried when over forty worshipers in the churches of Tanta suffered the same fate. And that atrocity had just happened when pilgrims near Minya, including many children, fell into the hands of Islamist murderers. Is it unfair, ultimately, to single out the Twenty-One and their fate from this long series of atrocities – gruesome acts it currently seems will continue into the future? This is a rebuke I heard from several Copts in Cairo, who accused the church of remaining silent about the many killings on Egyptian soil so as not to embarrass the government, and of emphasizing the Twenty-One simply because they were murdered abroad. I then tried to explain what I saw as the key difference between the many people shot or bombed and the Twenty-One: they had not only been defenselessly slaughtered, but they had audibly professed their faith in Jesus Christ just before and even during their decapitation.

Restricting my view to the Twenty-One, I refrain from speculating about the future of Copts in Egypt. Some may be left unsatisfied by my fatalistic view of current conditions, countering that we shouldn't resign ourselves to a permanent state of injustice and violence; after all, there are think tanks working hard to solve the world's problems. These thinkers, of course, would know exactly what questions to ask: Isn't there any way that the Coptic community and Islamic majority might eventually live in harmony? What kind of international peace conference,

United Nations intervention, peace mission, transnational roundtable, or moderated conflict resolution might take care of the "Coptic question"?

All this hand-wringing obscures a sense of despair bordering on the unintentionally comic. A degree of good will verging on self-denial, on both sides, would be the first condition of rapprochement, since the history of Copts and Arabs, Christians and Muslims, living alongside one another has had both worse and better times over the centuries, though no truly good chapters. The unresolved tension between Arab conquerors and vanquished Copts weighs heavily on present-day Egypt, though, honestly, the country has other hopeless situations as well. But violence isn't actually an option, probably not even for fanatical Islamists, because there are too many Copts to simply drive them all out or murder them. In other words, the Turkish solution for Armenians and Greeks is no longer on the table. And where would they be shipped off to, anyway? Over many centuries of Jewish diaspora, the Jews could always dream of their homeland in Israel. But the Copts are already living in their homeland, to which they lay a claim predating that of the Arabs.

The Copts' perseverance is all the more astonishing in light of the fact that such persistent pressures haven't caused them to crack. The Twenty-One displayed a similar steadfastness. On my journey to Upper Egypt I homed in on the places these martyrs had lived, orbiting them at both greater and lesser distances, hoping this approach might tell me something about those who can no longer speak for themselves.

Gaber

3

The Video

IT IS A SCRUPULOUSLY MADE SHORT FILM, shot with several cameras, and there's nothing amateurish about it. The beginning bodes well, opening with grace and even lightness. Arabic letters dance atop a black background, flowing as if afloat on a calmly whirling current of water, and finally come together, forming a droplet of closely intertwined characters. In Arabic calligraphy – one of Islam's most refined arts – an entire poem can be written as a single sign, which only a highly trained scribe can decode. This particular sign is the logo of one "Al Hayat Media Center." In this carefully choreographed film, everything has its place.

Then the name of President Obama appears, his middle name Hussein emphasized with capital letters. We are clearly meant to recall this Muslim name as Obama himself appears on screen. Known for his eloquence and delivery, reciting speeches smoothly as a clergyman or actor, he's shown in apparent distress, mourning the atrocities committed in the name of Jesus during the Crusades. The message is clear: in all of history, nothing is without consequence. Everything we're about to see is the answer to the president's contrite confession.

"A Message Signed with Blood to the Nation of the Cross": that's the title of the film in English. It is elegantly set in a classical typeface, with most letters in black; only the word "blood" is red. We hear the sound of waves and see a sandy beach, interspersed by rocky reefs. The sky is overcast, giving the few colors greater intensity and depth. Text appears, informing us that it is the "Coast of Wilayat Tarabulus," west of the Libyan port town of Sirte.

Then, from behind one of the rocky outcrops, a man in a bright orange jumpsuit slowly appears, his head bowed. His hands are tied behind his back and on his neck rests the hand of his captor, a black-clad giant whose face is hidden by a mask that leaves only his eyes visible. The two of them are not alone. They are followed by a long line of similar pairs in orange and black. The men swathed in black all look to be about a head taller than the men in orange.

The camera then zooms out, giving an overview of the entire scene. The procession unfolds, moving quietly – almost leisurely – forward. When a man in orange pauses at one of the rocky spots, his counterpart in black patiently waits until he has made his way over it, marking a shared moment, as if a farmer were helping his donkey over a small obstacle. A caption meanwhile instructs the viewer that these captives are "followers of the hostile Egyptian Church."

Now the camera zooms in on the men. They line up beside one another in a tightly packed row; this happens smoothly, as if rehearsed. No one is out of step. The sand is full of footprints – maybe this is where they practiced for the perfectly staged event? Clearly no improvisation was welcome in this film. Its simple script wouldn't allow for any lulls or blurred takes: not a single individual could break out of line, and there certainly couldn't be any visible resistance. Then, after a short pause, all the men in orange fall to their knees simultaneously, in a grim kind of chorus line. The men in black tower behind them, looking even taller than before, each holding his left hand on his captive's collar while his right fondles the handle of the dagger sheathed on his chest. There are twenty-one men in orange, one of them a dark-skinned Sub-Saharan African, so the lineup can be perfectly symmetrical – the sole black man kneels in the middle, and behind him stands the only captor not dressed in black, but in desert camouflage fatigues. His mask is pale yellow, the area around his mouth visibly moist from his breath.

The man in camo now addresses viewers in a speech. His English bears no discernible accent, which led many people to presume he was North American. But even if he were, he likely doesn't claim that citizenship any longer, since he is now a member of a larger, worldwide community. Whether the arrest of some of the captors in October 2017 will help clarify his identity remains to be seen. He begins his speech with "all praises due to Allah, the strong and mighty" – words reminiscent of the Greek Orthodox liturgy, which were in turn incorporated into Coptic liturgy: "Holy God, Holy One, Holy Immortal, have mercy on us," a prayer that long predates the Islamic conquest. His voice is calm, though he is fiercely accusatory. He blames Christians for launching one long war against Islam – a battle spanning from the Middle Ages to the present day. It is fitting that Obama's predecessor, George W. Bush, called the Iraq war a *crusade,* and that Obama decried the wrongs of medieval Crusaders. The spokesman in this video likely knows as little about the historical Crusades as any American president, but he's obviously more intent on proving the symmetry that justifies the use of this term: on one side stands the American crusade, pitting its Christian vassals against all Muslims; on the other, there is the answer of all Muslims – yes, really, every single Muslim, since he apparently aspires to speak for the entire community of believers. For him, this is a worldwide conflict, a battle to the very end. When the good side finally wins, the mercy of the All-merciful will be manifest, and He will finally bestow peace upon humankind.

The spokesman pauses now and then, as if trying to remember a well-rehearsed text. "Here we are, south of Rome" – he speaks like a military commander aiming to advance. Rome is the real enemy. The name "Rome" encapsulates everything that has resisted Islam – even though the Coptic Church wasn't involved in the Crusades, and to this day maintains independence from Rome and the Vatican; even though North America, which led the Iraq wars, has Christian sects that consider Rome the Whore of Babylon; and even though Arab rulers also participate – verbally, at least – in the ominous "war on terror." The speaker points the tip of his dagger at us, the video's viewers, but, despite this threatening gesture, his tone remains calm, unshakeable. He's keeping a tally, and it adds up: all previously spilled blood must be made up for by newly spilled blood. He himself is involved in the fight, of course, but at the same time refers to it all from an elevated viewpoint. "The sea in which you" – Americans, Christians, Romans? – "have hidden Sheikh Osama bin Laden's body, we swear to Allah we will mix it with your blood." Where there is justice, there is no room for fanaticism, and thus his conclusion sounds almost peaceful. He has put the dagger back into the sheath on his chest; his fingers play with the strings hanging from its handle. Now the camera zooms in on the sheath, foreshadowing the action about to happen.

The disciplined speech, clearly articulated through the fabric of his mask, is followed by an eloquent silence. Words like these, albeit unspoken, linger in the air: "You, who should watch this movie to the very end, are all – in your weak brutality and your immorally utilitarian thought – convinced that there is no one on earth whom you cannot buy or bribe. You believe that doing battle is always a question of where the greater economic advantage lies, and that your enemies will always leave a loophole open, another chance for you to try and make a deal. You believe that cruelty is unwise and detrimental to profit – unless you yourselves are the ones committing the atrocities. You hope that there are limits that even we dare not cross, because it would destroy all remaining common ground, making it impossible to patch things up and move on after the war. You believe that, in the end, everything will lead to endless conversations, and you feel safe on such terrain, because your constant lies help you debate everything to pieces in so-called negotiations. And that's precisely why a salutary stroke of terror now awaits you. Waking up from an illusory dream can be painful, but it brings you back to reality, and is therefore always good. And the step you currently view as an impossible leap of faith is actually quite small – it's easy to change the world forever. You'll experience firsthand how easy it is to do what you consider not just forbidden, but unthinkable. Once you understand this, you will come to know the majesty of terror. This terror shall crawl under your skin and never, ever leave you. From now on, you will know that your world has already perished – that, even where you believe you're surrounded by splendor and wealth, only shadows remain."

It's as if these unspoken words lie below the silent scene, whose staging is reminiscent of monks mutely lined up to enter a church in procession – an intentional pause for reflection that Christian monastic practice refers to as *statio*. The camera then scans over the faces of the kneeling men in orange jumpsuits. This clothing is part of the message: it evokes a scene now familiar worldwide – images of bound prisoners kneeling in cages, their heads bent low – a reference to Guantanamo, the offshore American military base in Cuba where the United States has permanently ruined its reputation as a nation that respects the rule of law.

The inextricable, increasingly unholy, long-festering conflict between the West and Islam, with its countless root causes, has grown on all sides into a longing for a simplistic storybook narrative. The myth begins with the collapse of the Twin Towers in New York. The following chapter features pictures of orange-uniformed inmates and scenes of torture from Abu Ghraib. Then we see President Obama and his secretary of state, Hillary Clinton, watching the screen spellbound as SEAL Team Six hunts Osama bin Laden. And now we have another chapter, another image, with which the other side aims to take the lead and make itself unforgettable.

The camera lingers on individual faces. For viewers who have only seen the prisoners' passport photos, not all of them are easy to identify; during captivity, previously shaven faces have grown bearded, and some men tilt their heads downward. On the left you can clearly see twenty-three-year-old Kiryollos with his questioning, almost absent-looking expression. The camera lingers on the face of twenty-two-year-old Gaber, whose brow is furrowed and whose eyes stay closed as his lips move in whispered prayer. Captivity has aged him; he looks like a forty-year-old. Ezzat, thirty-two, bends over as if something on the ground has caught his attention. Twenty-four-year-old Issam, whose fairer skin sets him apart, shifts a bit on his knees and turns his head to Matthew, who kneels beside him but does not return his gaze and merely stares straight ahead. One of the prisoners isn't kneeling upright like the others, but has sunk back onto his heels: Samuel (the younger), twenty-two, who looks the most like his passport photo. His youthful face, large eyes, and full lips show a fundamental, unflappable friendliness.

An eerie calm looms over the men. It has been suggested that the video's directors, who had to ensure that nothing interrupted the action, drugged their victims. Issam's watchful expression and movement, which make it look like he's ready to jump up, and Gaber's prayer both make me doubt it. Since none of them speaks a word of English, they can't have understood the speech. But the speaker's steady, self-assured voice probably tells them that not even a gun to the head could change this man's mind.

Then, in a synchronized wave, the captors push their bound prisoners forward, faces down in the sand. They loom over them, kneel atop their backs, grab their hair, pull their heads up, unsheathe their knives, and hold the blades to their throats. No one screams, only a jumble of soft voices is audible: *Ya Rabbi Yassou!* – "Oh my Lord Jesus!" – the quick prayer of the dying.

Most versions of the video still available today end here, but the original version posted online was also "cut" in this same spot – giving an otherwise technical film-editing term a gruesome connotation. Cutting the men's throats must not have gone as smoothly as hoped – perhaps some of the executioners had to hack away longer than planned to fully sever the cartilaginous trachea and neck – exposing a lack of professionalism that the propagandists who spread the news of this grisly crime wished to hide. Suddenly it becomes clear why Dr. Guillotin and his wretched contraption were once considered humanitarian.

But then the result appears: the executioners have set the severed heads on the backs of the corpses. At first glance, they look like they've sprouted up on the spot, a bunch of cut up and then wrongly reassembled bodies. Their faces, which the camera zooms in on, are disfigured in death. Their features look as if they're being pulled apart on all sides, and their skin, sun-tanned and healthy looking just a moment ago, is now a deathly pale yellow. Would these men's mothers still recognize their sons? Kiryollos's head is the only one that hasn't fully bled out, betraying nothing of the horrors that have just taken place. Did the director specially choose the head of this particular youth, who seems to be only sleeping, for this close-up? How might viewers ever reconcile his seemingly undisturbed peace with the cruel act that preceded it? Did some of the executioners have a poetic soul that inspired them to riff on the relationship between sleep and death?

The leader, having cut off the head of the Sub-Saharan African, ends the brief moment of reverie. He has risen from the corpse and stands up straight. Holding the knife in his bloodied hand, he again brandishes the tip toward the camera, as if to tell viewers: it's coming for your necks, too, until victory is ours.

And then the camera pans back to the sea, which laps as softly as before, though the water is no longer a grayish blue. Now it is reddened by one hundred liters of blood. The stain doesn't spread quickly, but grows like a cloud, gradually turning blue to red. This is only the beach of Sirte, but we get the message: this is what the sea will look like on countless coasts if the executioners get their way. Many perpetrators of political violence over the last hundred years have hoped that a new world and a new righteousness would emerge from such rivers of blood, but few have celebrated sheer bloodshed as much as these men on the beach of Wilayat Tarabulus.

Nietzsche once credited the famous French stage actor François-Joseph Talma, who practiced his imperial strut under Napoleon's guidance, with having concisely expressed the essence of all arts: "Everything that has to strike people as true must not be true." This video, despite its formal scrupulousness, makes the opposite case. This video is two things at once: both the documentation of a very real massacre and an allegory of the never-ending struggle between good and evil. Its directors certainly thought that they had cast the roles clearly, as each side wore its own distinctly colored uniform to this battle.

Doesn't the jumpsuits' garish orange unmistakably hint at the scandalous injustice of the "nation of the cross"?

But the anonymity of the masked murderers and the visible individuality of their victims thwart this effect. The faces of the prisoners clearly show that these young peasants could influence neither the American government nor any other, let alone their own. Their patience, their stoic dignity, and their prayers make them seem poor choices for casting as representatives of evil. Did the video's producers even consider the possibility that the weak and defenselessness Twenty-One might look neither contemptible nor miserable to viewers from the "nation of the cross"? Or that such viewers would definitely see it as a battle of good against evil, but with the roles reversed?

Indeed, the video's striking visuals are so memorable they have assumed a life of their own, and are now part of our collective imagination. None of the countless other Islamist murders will remain etched in our cultural memory as deeply as this one, above all because its directors gave it such a highly aestheticized form. With this video, they have achieved their aim: to render hatred visible. They have revived a specter the Western world thought it had overcome after its victory over Hitler: unconditional, uncompromising enmity; an enmity that can only be ended by the absolute annihilation of one of two opposing forces; an enmity that makes negotiations and peace conferences impossible. Evil has made its comeback, but it is not the "evil old enemy of yore," the enemy of humankind, *hostis humani generis*. It's an enmity not so much in the political sense as in the theological sense. After seeing this "Message Signed with Blood to the Nation of the Cross," it is no longer so easy to shut our eyes to the reality of such enmity.

Terror is often accompanied by triteness. In spring 2017 the Metro Cinema on Talaat Harb, a historic commercial street in Downtown Cairo, showed the film *Al-Armouti*

Fe Ard El-Nar ("The Return of Al-Armouti"), an Egyptian
farce starring a popular comedian. Al-Armouti has a big
belly, short legs, a bald head, and a huge mustache. He's a
simpleton, an analog of the Good Soldier Švejk of European
literary fame, and one of the cheerful disasters that befalls
him is being captured by Daesh, the death warriors of the
Islamic State. His executioners are dressed all in black, with
eye slits in the knit caps masking their faces, and Al-Armouti
wears the notorious orange jumpsuit on the way to his
execution. As the hatchet looms over his head – apparently
he's not to be slaughtered with the shorter knives used in
the original – an army arrives to save him. The men in black
fall amid rapid gunfire, and Al-Armouti is spared.

Laughter in the dark cinema proved people found the
scene funny. There's not a hint of real-world religious
conflict, the Egyptian civil war, or the cross – none of
that plays even the slightest part in this comedy – but
the symbolic weight of black and orange and the act of
beheading is so popular that satire could capitalize on it.
In my native Germany such a spoof would probably be less
well received, as "mocking the victims" will always invite
reproach; but, given the depressing situation in Egypt, I was
inclined to be more forgiving. For Egyptians living under a
military dictatorship that, severe as it may be, won't likely
manage to end the slaughter of its minority Christian population, the impulse to laugh the horrors off with a night at
the movies is somehow understandable. I can only hope
this particular comedy won't make it as far as the villages
of Upper Egypt, where the martyrs were from.

Bishoy

4

A Conversation about Martyrdom

SHORTLY AFTER MY ARRIVAL in Egypt I went to Zahret Al-Bustan, a teahouse in downtown Cairo frequented by literati, where I met a young man from an Arab family. He readily told me about himself, outlining his life story and saying he feels equally at home in Europe and North Africa. His parents were communists and had distanced themselves from Islam; he grew up in England and had no contact with religion. He then moved back to Cairo, where he founded a software start-up. The company was still young, but he didn't come to this shabby teahouse to save money; he came because it was a better place for good conversation than the more famous Café Riche nearby, where the stuck-up staff tended to show scruffy-looking writers the door. But then he wanted to know what brought me to Egypt. When I told him about the Twenty-One, his expression showed disapproval.

"What is it about martyrs that fascinates you?"

Had we known one another longer, I might have dared confess what really appealed to me: the possibility of turning – in one swift moment – a life full of mistakes, humiliations, half-heartedness, and dishonesty into a meritorious life by making one simple declaration, a declaration made countless times before and which, if one were to live longer, could be made countless more times but which, upon death, became one's sole, final important act. Everything one had been in life would then be distilled down to this last detail, which then counted more than everything else. Martyrdom seemed to be a uniquely positive omen, morphing a misguided life into a holy prophesy. Did I stay silent so as not to reveal this shrewd calculation of mine?

We went on to talk of other things, but I later found myself thinking about how the conversation might have developed had I not avoided the topic altogether. It would have been difficult to convince the young entrepreneur to see things my way, but maybe I could have at least made him think it over. In this imagined conversation, I dubbed him "The Doubter" and myself "The Believer."

THE DOUBTER: I always feel uneasy when I hear the word *martyr*. In this part of the world people constantly talk about martyrs – every criminal who dons a suicide vest and kills at least twenty people is a martyr. Even the soldiers who died in the war against Israel are considered martyrs in Egypt, and are buried in a special "martyrs' cemetery." To me the word is just propaganda, a glorification of violence. It should be forbidden to speak of "martyrs"; the term is laden with too many lies.

THE BELIEVER: But you probably also know that Christians, who came up with the term, applied it to neither violent nor suicidal people; to them, it meant those who, even under threat of death, were unwilling to give up their faith.

THE DOUBTER: Of course I know that! But it's still a glorification of violence – be it actively exercised or passively endured. Violence is a social evil that must be fought; making its victims heroes and saints doesn't help.

Celebrating a martyr's holiness is one way of ensuring that violence is ever-present: it sticks in our minds and, in a perverse way, is even celebrated. A cult is built around the initial crime, keeping it perpetually alive, to the detriment of society. Egypt is so fragile right now – do you really think celebrating these martyrs contributes to the country's stability? It just sparks further aggressions, triggering hostility from the Christians, who incessantly apportion blame, and from the Muslims, who are perpetually blamed.

THE BELIEVER: But doesn't the sheer steadfastness of the Twenty-One make any impression on you? These were poor people who had a hard life – people from a completely ignored socioeconomic class, with no education, who lived hand-to-mouth. Where did they get such strength? They had no easy means to improve their living conditions, and yet they were strong enough to refuse to betray their faith.

THE DOUBTER: Who knows the motives underlying what you call steadfastness and strength, which might just as well have been stubbornness or defiance or a self-destructive taste for suffering? And what about peer pressure? Some of them might have wanted to save their own lives, but didn't dare step out of line.

THE BELIEVER: That's all speculation. No one can see into the hearts of the dead. If you have no evidence others acted in bad faith, you should assume they acted in good faith. It's too easy to suggest that their actions were rooted in defiance or vanity rather than a love of truth. Then, of course, such actions would deserve no merit.

THE DOUBTER: You call adherence to faith and religion a merit? My parents had faith, too – faith in communism – but they wouldn't have given their lives for it. They chose exile in England instead, where they live ten times better than they ever could have here. I profess no faith, but I do know that two plus two equals four: that's the truth, but surely you can't think I'd give my life for it! If a gun were held to my head, I'd be willing to swear that two plus two equals five, and anyone else would do the same.

THE BELIEVER: But the Twenty-One weren't asked to deny that two plus two equals four! Christianity's concept of truth is not a mathematical formula.

THE DOUBTER: Truth? Don't even get me started . . . ! You know what my truth is? Life! I enjoy every day to the hilt. I'm building my company. I'm in love with a beautiful girl. We'd already be married if I had enough money to buy an apartment, but I have my eye on one in Zamalek, one of Cairo's best neighborhoods. My parents are thrilled and have already signed for it. Tomorrow I'm off to Dubai, where I have a partner connecting me with a bank. See, things are moving forward. Life! There's nothing else. What did your martyrs experience? What had they seen? I was in London when I was twenty – I don't need to spell out for you what that means. I've never been to Upper Egypt, and never will go, because ancient ruins bore me to tears, but even more because people there are unbelievably primitive – their main concern is procreation. Your martyrs threw away a life they hadn't even lived. The younger ones had probably never even had a woman! All they saw of Libya were construction sites – they hadn't experienced a thing, they hadn't really lived. Being clueless to the point of complete ignorance is the main requirement for martyrdom. Admit it.

THE BELIEVER: You overestimate the wealth of your experiences and adventures. Each of us only gets to see a tiny slice of a vast reality. The martyrs lived within rather limited horizons, no doubt, but that says nothing about the intensity of their experiences. Happiness, passion, amazement, and joy are emotional states that can be sparked even by the smallest stimuli, and extend to one's very soul. I wouldn't be so sure, if I were you, that you've enjoyed life so much more than them just because you've been to London drug parties. These men had nothing to lose – but isn't that a rather unimaginative way of seeing things? Can't you picture a perspective from which your own existence would seem stodgy and narrow-minded? To put it another way, must one have exhausted all the pleasures life has to offer in order to know how exquisitely precious it is?

THE DOUBTER: But that makes their willingness to die even more incomprehensible. Everyone knows that an admission made under threat of death carries no weight. The inquisitor is always the dupe. Galileo could easily recant, precisely because he knew he was right. His truth stood completely independent of his forced statement: the earth's orbit around the sun didn't change when he told the inquisitors what they wanted to hear.

THE BELIEVER: I'm glad you mention the worthlessness of a confession made under threat of death. In Galileo's case your argument is apt – but what if the confession involves betraying another person? As you rightly argue, the person being threatened or blackmailed can't be considered at fault, but if he survives he'll never be able to forgive himself.

THE DOUBTER: But that's not the case here. Your martyrs, if I've understood it right, weren't under any pressure to betray their fellows. It was about their religion, and theirs was as much a figment of the imagination as the murderers'. They weren't real believers if they couldn't trust their own truth, independent of any confession and regardless of any posturing.

THE BELIEVER: As I've already pointed out, the Christians' concept of truth is not a mathematical formula, and has nothing to do with Galileo's description of the earth's orbit around the sun. . . .

THE DOUBTER: I'd be curious to hear about this special concept of truth you keep referring to.

THE BELIEVER: The Christians' concept of truth is neither formula nor doctrine – it is a person, Jesus Christ, who said that he himself is the truth. Those to whom he has revealed himself must not, and cannot, ever betray him; they must instead bear witness to his simultaneous divinity and humanity. Christianity has holy books, the Gospels, which can be appreciated even by the nonreligious, but the Gospels alone can't explain the rapid spread of the Christian religion. The secret behind the religion's expansion are the people who, from the very start, were ready to die for their love of Jesus: martyrs. There were many, especially in Egypt. Even before the Gospels were written, and long before the first councils sought to establish a theological definition of faith in Jesus Christ as Savior, martyrs were already bearing witness to his status; later on, the theologians merely ratified the martyrs' faith. Scientific and philosophical truth is proved by exhaustive, conclusive reasoning. Christians' truth, on the other hand, is proved by their readiness to die for it.

THE DOUBTER: That may well have been the case, although I find such an idea disagreeable, even a bit creepy. Bearing witness to something you've never seen? Luckily we're long past that. At any rate, I've never met the kind of Christian you're talking about. London is full of churches, and their bells ring all across the city every Sunday morning. You see people coming out of Mass, but none of them would think of getting a cross tattooed on their hands like the Copts do, to provoke others with their faith. In London people are discreet about religion; they don't rub your face in it. And the Copt I'm going to buy the apartment from, a hardcore businessman with major investments in New Cairo, isn't the kind of Christian you're describing. For him, business is the ultimate truth, which I totally get. It sounds like your peasants from those dumps in Upper Egypt might be the very last Christians.

THE BELIEVER: At the moment it may seem so. But if the phrase from the early North African church still holds true – that "the blood of the martyrs is the seed of the church" – then perhaps the Twenty-One should not be counted among the very last Christians, but rather among the first.

Samuel (the younger)

5

The Martyrs' Bishop

IN THE UPPER EGYPTIAN CITY of Samalut, the diocesan headquarters near the martyrs' home village of El-Aour, no one gives much thought to the fact that the city is an ancient settlement dating back to the dawn of human civilization. My Cairo-based friend Mohammed, a young defense attorney who is also the son of a local farmer, had left for the city as soon as he could. He was surprised when I told him my plans. Having swiftly adopted a degree of big-city arrogance, he now looks down on his rural roots, and couldn't believe that I would want to go there, of all places. "Samalut, Samalut," he exclaimed over and over again, shaking his head, bemused, "that's crazy!" For him, the very name of his hometown had something hilarious about it – nothing in the world could make him venture back there.

At first glance, the city looked no worse than many others I'd passed through with the young deacon who had brought me here from Cairo. On its outskirts, where the first dilapidated concrete buildings stood, the pavement came to an abrupt end. Our car rumbled on down the bumpy dirt road, and both potholes and traffic increased. Pedicabs, known locally as *tuk-tuks*, wove between trucks without the slightest worry of being crushed, despite the obvious likelihood of such accidents. Apparently, Cairo's *tuk-tuk* drivers are not the only ones known for their drug use, and although it might calm their nerves, it certainly doesn't make them more attentive. When we were suddenly out of the crowd again and I asked where the city center had been, the only reply was a perplexed expression on the face of my traveling companion.

City center? I immediately understood that my question revealed I was a European, with traditional European ideas of urban structure, even though European cities are also growing increasingly formless. A main market square, town hall, cathedral, castle, and guild halls – no such framework, which might make a city recognizable as a political entity to Western eyes, could be found here. Samalut was not a *polis,* and never had been.

Conversely, the city's most impressive buildings sought invisibility: the vast grounds around the new cathedral included the archbishopric's school, guesthouse, and hospital, as well as the metropolitan bishop's residence. All these structures disappeared behind high walls, heavily guarded by police and soldiers, forming an island of cleanliness and order replete with tournament swimming pools for the students and a cafeteria where even Muslim girls could be seen, as it was the only public place unaccompanied women were allowed to visit.

Where did all the dapper young people around the pool, dressed in Western clothes, come from? Did they live in the multistory, slightly crooked concrete buildings lining the surrounding streets, behind small windows whose dirty panes were carelessly draped with dismal rags? There were no other neighborhoods around here, at least as far as I could see. Not that I could really explore – as soon as I had entered the circumscribed area under the metropolitan's care, I was hardly allowed to leave on my own. Armed guards kept me from wandering off, as it was "too dangerous." Locals weren't used to the sight of Westerners, and their distrust could easily escalate into irritation.

I repeatedly detected a tense mood throughout my trip, although I never felt it was directed against me as a visiting foreigner. Generally speaking, Egyptians are not noisy people – aside from bouts of blaring car horns, deafening music played at religious festivals, and sermons from mosques broadcast out over the streets. They rarely speak in raised voices, which makes it all the more disturbing when the occasional sudden outburst occurs in a crowd – a brief rant, scuffle, back-and-forth pushing, or high-volume outrage – only to sink back into near silence, like a short flame flaring up in bone-dry brushwood during a drought.

This was true even in the church-run hospital of Samalut. The metropolitan had procured cutting-edge equipment for this new facility, and was so proud of it that he let one of his fellows give me a tour. Its stairways and corridors were swamped with patients from all over the province who sat on the floor in rustic robes, waiting to see a doctor.

In the intensive care unit, a man of about forty had just died. Seven men in long *jellabiya*, the loose robes traditionally worn here, were circled around his deathbed, where he lay with outstretched arms and spread legs, as if he had just fallen from the sky, his eyes still open. The men were agitated, crying, talking to each other, and one had thrown himself onto the bed with the corpse – apparently this death had surprised them all. As their emotions intensified they spoke louder, and then the man who had lain over the corpse and covered it with kisses let go, jumped up, and unleashed a fit of rage. He tore around the room, ripping open cabinets of medical records, tossing papers into the air, making threats, and throwing a chair at the glass door, which shattered. Finally, he let himself be stopped by his companions, who grabbed hold of him and led him away.

The Coptic doctor, a youthful man going gray at the temples, had calmly watched the entire scene. The mourner's destructive fit didn't bother him in the least – on the contrary, it seemed he found such a reaction to death entirely appropriate, and rather common. The people of Upper Egypt can be sensitive and passionate, but are equally quick to return to more peaceful states. The dead man was then taken away, to be wrapped in a shroud and buried within the next few hours, as is the custom here.

My guide through the hospital was a young pharmacist originally from a village neighboring the martyrs' hometown, and currently on leave from his job in Saudi Arabia. As we were leaving the hospital he said he wanted to clarify what we'd just witnessed – such outbursts were related to pressures felt locally and nationally. Since the overthrow of Mubarak's dictatorship in 2011, the irreconcilable differences between the Muslim Brotherhood on the one hand and the moderate factions, including the Copts, on the other, have become increasingly clear to everyone. Any hope of reconciliation or peaceful reorganization now strikes many as utterly futile. The only thing keeping the country together is the fact that its new ruler, General el-Sisi, won't hesitate to use force.

I heard people voicing a similar hopelessness over and over again. But when I thought of the serenity with which the Coptic doctor had handled the shocked mourner in the ICU, all of a sudden I could also picture the Coptic Church of Egypt helping to heal the country – at least in places where it is as powerful as in Upper Egypt, with strong believers like this doctor.

The time had come for my audience with the metropolitan. First and foremost, I planned to request his help finding the martyrs' families. But now another question came to mind. The stateliness of his episcopal headquarters amazed me. Hadn't I read that the Egyptian government was preventing Copts from building new churches? Hadn't several churches all across Egypt been set ablaze after

President Mubarak was overthrown, and hadn't Copts been beaten and murdered? The rising violence had made headlines even in Western news media.

But Western media somehow hadn't noticed that, alongside the rise in violence, a construction boom had begun. It was a building frenzy of the sort Coptic Christians hadn't experienced for over a thousand years: large new churches were sprouting up everywhere, some with towers taller than nearby minarets; new monasteries housed the many monks and nuns; ancient churches were extensively restored; and not all new buildings were strictly religious, as many schools and hospitals were also built. The new palace of the Metropolitan of Samalut stood opposite the unfinished cathedral, bastions of order in the midst of a chaotically growing city that guidebooks just a few years ago had referred to as a village.

A receptionist with bottle-blond, uncovered hair and tight jeans showed me up the wide main staircase, its bronze bannister cast to resemble a lush grapevine. Was her appearance, an unusual sight for a woman in an official position in this country, perhaps some kind of statement? I knew the metropolitan had written a much-debated book on the role of women in the church.

His Eminence received me in a marble hall adorned with the kind of faux flower bouquets one would see in a hotel lounge. He sat far from the folding doors, on a leather armchair at the front of the room; it wasn't a throne, but was positioned like one. He had a low desk in front of him and a telephone at his side, which he occasionally picked up and quietly spoke into. His right hand held a golden cross since, as bishop, he was always ready to bless people – that was his real function. His full lips, bright eyes, and pale, smooth skin made him look youthful despite his white beard. After initially studying medicine, he had been ordained early on as bishop, and he had held this high office for forty years already.

I received a rather cool reception. Naturally, he did not rise to greet me, and after a brief examination his large eyes seemed to gaze straight through me. A slight movement of the hand holding the cross was his invitation for me to speak.

"I was hoping to write about the twenty-one martyrs, and would like to meet their families and get better acquainted with the circumstances surrounding their lives. . . ."

His blank expression made me uncertain. As I spoke he used a mechanism in the armrest of his chair to raise the footrest and lower his back – I couldn't help but think of the imperial Byzantine throne in Constantinople, upon which reverent visitors saw their emperor rise into the air. I later learned that the metropolitan was merely trying to mitigate his severe back pain by occasionally changing his posture. After a moment of silence, he began to speak in a skeptical, almost ironic tone.

"Why do you want to meet these people? Do not expect too much. They are all the same. You can visit any Coptic family, and you will find the same attitude toward the church everywhere – the same strong faith, and the same readiness for martyrdom. This is not a Western church in a Western society. We are the Church of Martyrs. I take no special risk when I say that not a single Copt in Upper Egypt would betray the faith."

He made no attempt to hide the certainty of his superiority. It seemed likely that he had encountered Western Christians who approached him with the conviction that they could impress and perhaps even teach the representative of a church that had neither a Hagia Sophia nor a Cologne Cathedral, a church that had experienced neither Rudolf Bultmann's demythologization nor any liturgical reform. To be sure, my attitude was nothing of the sort:

from the very start, I was genuinely prepared to admire everything I was to discover in the Coptic world.

I managed to bring him from generalities back to the Twenty-One of his own diocese. The metropolitan had been involved in their canonization, and knew each case as it was filed.

"We find ourselves in the odd position of being grateful to the Islamist killers for the film with which they documented their acts. Now, instead of relying on potentially contradictory testimonies, we can see it all with our own eyes. Had the killers had any idea of the significance this video would have for the Coptic Church, they probably would not have made it. Far from being intimidating, it gives us courage. It shows us the martyrs' heroic bravery, and the fact that they spent their last moments alive in prayer proves the strength of their faith."

He paused, as if to ensure his words had an effect on me.

Nobody knows what happened in the days leading up to the killings, but there were reports regarding the evening, or rather the night, of their capture. There were other workers staying in the same house, but they had managed to escape. They had grown suspicious when they heard their names being called from the darkness. Someone must have given the murderers the workers' names. They were probably already asleep when someone outside began calling, "Abanub," "Kiryollos," "Samuel."

A name being called out in the dark – where had I read something like this before? Wasn't there a story in the Old Testament about a sleeping young man awakened one night when he heard his name being called? He, too, was named Samuel. He awoke and said, "Here I am." In the Vulgate, the Latin term is *adsum,* which has become the answer Catholic candidates for ordination give when the bishop asks whether they are ready to become a priest. In the Bible, Samuel is called three times, until he realizes that the voice calling him is no mere human voice. And although the Coptic Samuel wouldn't have said *"adsum"* as he ran out of the house and into his murderer's hands, he was nevertheless ready; he had pronounced his own *adsum* long ago, over and over, and now the time had come for it to truly count.

Conversing with Copts about their martyrs invariably involves allusions to the Bible – in their eyes, everything that happens is a reflection, fulfillment, or repetition of biblical events. They are so close to the books of the Old and New Testaments, it's as if two millennia hadn't passed in the meantime. Might their ability to tap into this kind of timelessness stem from some continuation of Egyptian antiquity, as if time had simply held its breath for nearly three thousand years? Historically speaking, following the end of Roman persecution, the schism at the Council of Chalcedon, and the Islamic conquest, the Copts have also been unaffected by the many forces that have shaped the Western church: no Reformation, no Counter-Reformation, no secularization. The Coptic Church, situated as it is – in the ongoing, sometimes more oppressive, sometimes gentler stranglehold of Islamic authority – has long seemed doomed to a slow death.

"From the very start, our coexistence with Muslim Arabs was forced. And, according to the laws of history, the future holds no more unity than the present. How could we ever become one, as long as Muslims are Muslims and Christians are Christians? And we intend to remain Christians – or should the unity of this country be more important than its peoples' faith?"

It was a rhetorical question, offered as the chair's footrest rose even higher.

"The Arab invasion was a land grab, but land grabs only succeed if the invaders can convince the vanquished to accept their religion and culture. We would never even consider that. We Copts are the real, true Egyptians. This has been our land for many thousands of years – it was our land long before the pyramids were built. We have an ironclad, far-reaching memory. Our memory is at least as good as the Jews', who to this day have not forgiven Pharaoh, and always remember that God gave them the land of the Canaanites back in Moses' day: two thousand years later, they took it back. That's why Muslims hate talking about history. They find the idea that they aren't the beginning of everything dangerous, so for them the notion that what came before wasn't just darkness and idolatry is unthinkable. But our situation is different from that of the Jews. We've become a minority in our own country, even if we aren't as much of a minority as the government would like."

I was curious to hear what number he would cite, because I had been hearing several different, constantly higher figures. But he didn't want to get into numbers.

"We are a quarter of the population – and I consciously avoid saying 'people' because there are several peoples in Egypt. We wouldn't want to forget the Bedouins and Nubians, many of whom, although they aren't Copts, are Christians." It's difficult for politicians to clarify matters in this regard. If one admits to such a high proportion of Christians, then denying the Copts their basic rights would be impossible, no matter how hard one might try. "Church records document all baptisms, which gives us a reliable overview."

The uninhibited manner in which he spoke was contrasted by his physical rigidity, which, when I learned of his back pain, I decided to interpret as an involuntary expression of self-control. The longer the audience lasted, the more my initial impression that he belonged to a persecuted, marginalized church faded. By no means would he let the lack of civil rights and the pogrom-like attacks on churches and believers fall by the wayside, but he also refused to complain that the church was weak, perhaps because he himself felt strong, or perhaps because he considered whining and lamenting unworthy of his station as leader of his people. It seemed to me as if his position with respect to the country's rulers was like that of a player seated at a chess board, and that as the royal game was played, his hands were in no way tied behind his back.

I now broached the subject of the many legal obstacles that had to be overcome in Egypt to build any new church facility. How could he explain the abundance of magnificent new churches – not just in his diocese, but in so many others as well?

That was the first and only time the serious expression briefly vanished from his face. He didn't offer any explanations, and I was left to guess at a message he didn't care to spell out. Reading between the lines, I surmised that in a country like this, laws are one thing, while their enforcement is something else entirely. The absence of the rule of law can often benefit those who know how to navigate it.

But what of the martyrdom of his fellow Copts, especially the Twenty-One? In his eyes, it proved one thing above all else: the power of the church. I reflected on how amusing it would be to see Friedrich Nietzsche – with his concept of Christianity as a religion of resentment, a slaves' religion – square off against this particular priest. The Christian hospital he founded is the largest and most modern in all of Upper Egypt, and employs many Muslim doctors. As a doctor himself, this accomplishment lay particularly close to his heart, but then there were the schools, too, to which Muslim students also flocked. Such initiatives secured the church an enduring place among public institutions, and it was impossible to picture life here without them.

"The church does what the government cannot."

He adjusted the back of his chair and held the cross, which hadn't left his hand the entire time, toward me so I could give it a kiss. He did so without the kindly, affectionate smile with which the powerful in the West seek the approval of their subjects. Here stood the absolute archetype of a pragmatic, forward-looking reactionary – a kind of leader utterly unknown in the West – in undisputed greatness.

وَلَمَّا فَتَحَ الْخَتْمَ الْخَامِسَ. رَأَيْتُ تَحْتَ الْمَذْبَحِ نُفُوسَ الَّذِينَ قُتِلُوا مِنْ أَجْلِ كَلِمَةِ اللهِ وَمِنْ أَجْلِ الشَّهَادَةِ الَّتِي كَانَتْ عِنْدَهُمْ. (رؤ ٦:٩)

الشهيد
عزت بشرى نصيف
ولد ١٤-٨-١٩٨٢
استشهدا فى ليبيا يوم ١٦-٢-٢٠١٥

Ezzat

6

The Martyrs' Pilgrimage Church

THE JOURNEY TO EL-AOUR began where the city of Samalut fell off like a cardboard box that had burst at the seams. All around spread a broad plain of verdant fields – modern farms growing semi-dwarf wheat. This green sea was dotted with island-like villages whose tallest points were domed towers topped by crosses. Mosque minarets became a less frequent sight. At first glance, this appeared to be thoroughly Coptic terrain.

We started out following a canal that ran straight as an arrow, which we soon crossed, and then continued along down a dirt road. I was traveling with a local guide, as there was no way I could have found the families on my own. There were no street signs. Even if there had been, I wouldn't have been able to read them. Each village looked the same as the next, at first, but then an unexpected sight caught my eye: amid a cluster of buildings on the horizon, a gigantic, round, white structure stood out. A nuclear reactor, perhaps? As we drew closer, it became clear: this mighty concrete dome, curving from the ground upward, was no reactor, but its massive size dwarfed the many buildings crowded around it. Not just the houses, but even the steeple of the old parish church in the middle of the village seemed small and fragile in comparison.

Beside me sat Abuna Makar, the pastor of El-Aour, in a turban-shaped, black felt hat. He looked a bit displeased, as if he weren't too keen about his task. Even when we were with the bishop he had maintained a respectful, slightly bowed posture, as if to imply that he couldn't imagine how visiting these families would actually be of any use. Was he afraid too much attention would somehow jeopardize the village's fragile equilibrium, after all the trials and tribulations its people had already been through?

We looked at the giant dome – construction was still underway all around it. Egyptian president General el-Sisi had ordered the construction of this pilgrimage church to commemorate the martyrs. It was paid for by the government and, besides St. Mark's Cathedral in Cairo, would be one of the very few Coptic churches (if not the only one) built with Egyptian tax money. Unlike Islam, Egypt's official state religion, the Coptic Church does not receive government funding.

The general had been forced to give a clear sign of sympathy for the Egyptian citizens murdered abroad, and this building was its manifestation. Precariously positioned between both sides of the civil war, he felt dependent on the approval of the Copts. Might a magnificent church in which to honor their martyrs help put them at ease?

Meanwhile, the noteworthy structure has gained still greater significance. When it was planned in 2015, the martyrs' bodies were still missing. "The murderers threw them into the sea, where fish ate their remains," was more or less how I heard it told by the young deacon the pastor had brought along. It was a somewhat childish idea, since human bodies aren't easy to dispose of, but the ongoing civil war in Libya made it impossible to investigate any further. And then, in October 2017, the bodies were finally found: they had been buried in the desert not far from the scene of the massacre. Their hands were still tied behind their backs, their jumpsuits stained with blood.

For the Coptic Church it was immediately clear that the remains would have to be brought home. Pope Tawadros II of Alexandria called on the Egyptian government to lobby Libya for their return. He eventually succeeded, and in May 2018 a private jet flew the bodies of the twenty Egyptians to Cairo. (The body of Matthew, the Ghanaian, was not with them.) From there, the martyrs' remains were brought to El-Aour and laid to rest according to the solemn rites for handling sacred relics. The house of worship built in their memory then became a sepulchral church, granting it an even more exceptional status among Egyptian churches.

Would the bones be buried in sarcophagi? I was told Copts actually keep the relics of their saints in heavy wooden cylinders, which the priest holds for worshipers to kiss, and also holds to their heads, because Copts believe in maintaining physical contact with their saints. Other churches would certainly want relics of the new martyrs, too, so they might well be divided up and sent to several places. In any case, I hope my comparison of the pilgrimage church to an atomic reactor will not strike Coptic ears as disrespectful; after all, the high dome of their new church now holds, in the form of the martyrs' bodies, a sacred glowing core from which their faith radiates far and wide.

According to the Orthodox viewpoint, icons of the saints are almost as venerable as relics. Pope Tawadros canonized the Twenty-One just weeks after their murder. They were in any case considered *santi subito* – "saints straightaway" – because, according to old Christian custom, anyone who has borne witness to one's faith in Jesus Christ with one's own blood is worthy of sainthood, even if the life led prior to that point was less than holy. Now churches can be built and consecrated in their name,

and there can also be icons of them in which their heads
are surrounded by a halo or nimbus.

A widespread icon created shortly after February 15,
2015, shows the Twenty-One in a stylized, neo-archaic
composition: they're depicted kneeling so close together
that their halos overlap each other, hands raised toward an
image of Christ hovering above. Iconographically speaking,
this places them squarely within the well-established,
ancient tradition for portraying martyrs, and therefore
deliberately pays no heed to the men's actual appearance,
which would be well known through photographs. It is
done in the vein of a generalized, large-eyed, iconic archetype that virtually forbids any portrayal of unique traits.
Individuals' facial features belong to the transient realm
of human mortals, whereas icons show saints dwelling in
the sacred beyond. The fact that the Twenty-One are not
recognizable in detail on this icon thus confirms the high
rank to which they are destined.

Understandably, some of the martyrs' many relatives and
neighbors in El-Aour found the new icon unsatisfying – it
showed their sons, husbands, cousins, and brothers in
mannequin-like uniformity, one man indistinguishable
from the next. They wanted recognizable pictures of them.
And so a countermovement to the official liturgical art
sprang up, producing images that met both requirements:
"unofficial" icons that were recognizable to relatives, but
still suited to ritual worship by fellow faithful who had
never met them – pictures that served both as personal
portraits and devotional images.

I had gotten no farther than the outside courtyard of the
new martyrs' pilgrimage church when I came upon a poster
that had obviously been photoshopped, by a designer who
is likely to remain anonymous but whose work has since
spread through the whole of Coptic Egypt. He has taken
the men's heads from old photo IDs and placed them on

other bodies – a process that somehow echoes the theme
of beheading – standing ramrod straight, dressed in
white liturgical robes, a deacon's red stole crossing their
chests. Each has been granted the honor of this garment,
including those the bishop hadn't expressly appointed as
choristers – even Matthew, although we don't know whether
he had ever attended a Coptic Mass, or if he first learned
Coptic chants during their shared captivity. The martyrs'
hands, which aren't really theirs, hold crosses of the sort a
bishop uses to bless his congregation; on their heads perch
regal crowns whose two-dimensionality contrasts with the
photographic faces underneath, looking instead like gold
paper cut-outs.

I soon discovered countless variations of these martyr-
as-crowned-priest pictures: some showed all the men
together like a royal band standing before a pale blue sky
with little white clouds hovering amid painted angels;
others showed them with a cut-and-paste, American-style
Christ, his head lowered in mourning; still others had a
Russian-looking, enthroned Christ Pantocrator – ruler of
all – in the middle. And for each of these curious variants
several sub-variations had been created as well. I saw their
crowned photo-ID portraits amid painted angels and
saints, but there were also versions that had taken their still
images from the video, uniting them as sublime, crowned
saints in orange jumpsuits.

Comparing these reworked images with the vividly
colored stills from the original video, which show most
of the kneeling men with dark complexions and beards, it
becomes clear how heavily their photos were manipulated
to produce the crowned images. This group of hard-
laboring, deeply tanned farmhands and masons are shown
with pearl-white, rosy-cheeked skin and all blemishes
removed. The photo editor has made a valiant effort to give
them an air of purity and transfiguration, inadvertently

taking them halfway toward meeting the traditional iconic ideal. Each of these posters, foil-printed wall coverings, and postcards combines authenticity with exaggeration, souvenir photo with holy image.

They are, of course, rather less tasteful than the neo-archaic icons with which the Coptic Church formally welcomes its martyrs into the great choir of saints, putting them on par with the famous saints of a thousand years ago: monks, mystics, and miracle workers. For a church that has staunchly guarded itself from outside influence, these visuals force it to grapple with a problem of religious imagery that the West has been facing since the nineteenth century, perhaps without even realizing it. Does contemporary ecclesiastical art really only have two choices: colorless craftsmanship or cloying cliché?

To oversimplify things a little, one might well say that the bourgeoisie, which is less closely linked to the church, prefers artistic craftsmanship, whereas the pious and prayerful tend to find what they need in sticky-sweet images. In any case, these posters and postcards have oddly succeeded: they render the men who died in such agony recognizable, while at the same time bestowing on them a perfection that both satisfies the faithful and conforms to the tradition of the church. What Western artists – pop, video, and photoshop artists in particular – have long tried to achieve by embracing kitsch, thinking that old crafts could help them attain goals lost to "high art," has been achieved here, deep in what many would call a provincial backwater, by a computer novice: the creation of useful devotional images that help fulfill a serious spiritual need.

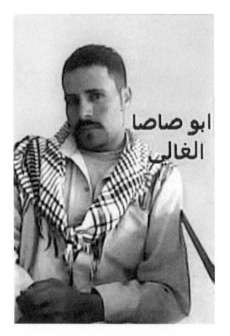

ابو صاصا
الغالي

Milad

7

The Martyrs' Village

ACCORDING TO MY FRIEND MOHAMMED, the defense lawyer from Cairo, fifty years ago the average Egyptian village – anywhere in the Nile Delta, the Faiyum Oasis, or even Upper Egypt – was a sought-after destination for city dwellers from Cairo and Alexandria. Then he corrected himself: "That was still the case even thirty years ago!"

His eyes lit up as he talked. It was as if he, who had never left Egypt, was trying to conjure up images from a journey into a vanished world.

This was true of every village, he said, since they were all the same. No wonder: construction techniques had long been the same almost everywhere in Egypt. Adobe bricks were still being used, as they had been for five thousand years; for this period, stretching as long as humankind's cultural memory, the standard building design in this region hadn't changed much. Clay was dug straight from the ground, kneaded with chopped straw, shaped into bricks, and dried in the sun for a few days. It wasn't the most durable building material, but it was easy to replace. Pots were made of the same clay; the biblical notion that Adam was made of clay by the divine potter probably originated here.

"These adobe houses stayed warm in winter and cool in summer," my friend continued. "Their rooms had fairly high ceilings, although they were also dark; only a few small windows faced the street, so most of the light came from the internal courtyards. The decorative touches built from adobe bricks – friezes, ornate frames and borders, cornices – helped even the humblest abode look stately."

Mohammed had been born in such a house. He recalled it being gorgeous, as beautiful as all the neighboring houses – there hadn't been any ugly ones. The door in the middle of the façade was designed as a grand entrance even in modest buildings. When the walls eventually crumbled back into a fine umber dust, the house, always the same yet always new, was rebuilt from fresh bricks. These houses had flat rooftops with roof terraces, and sometimes a second story. Their earthen floors were slightly uneven, and beneath them was the household cistern. Water was pumped, and the amount needed for day-to-day tasks was stored in a large amphora set within a round niche in the entrance hall. Mohammad's description reminded me of Italian Renaissance houses, in which utilitarian household objects were also well-designed, aesthetically pleasing gems.

I had heard, too, how these villages were full of trees in which all sorts of birds cavorted: sparrows sprang like confetti thrown into the air; there were hoopoes, considered messengers of love, and cattle egrets with dazzling white plumage. The canals running along the village edge were kept clean, and the streets were swept.

How was it possible, I wondered, for the traditional Egyptian village, in all its thousandfold variations, to vanish so completely? And so thoroughly: it disappeared nationwide, everywhere, including in El-Aour and its neighboring villages. It was still right before Mohammed's eyes, in a sense, but in reality it no longer existed. In a country whose public administration is so poorly organized, where the government does so little, where big plans fail and attempts at reform peter out, it's hard to see how something of the sort could take place. The government could never have set out to demolish and uniformly remake every single Egyptian village, and so successfully wipe out the past. It was as if all the country's villagers, all at once, and without expressly agreeing, had been overcome by a desire to dispose of their old dwellings and replace traditional building styles with a new uniformity that I can't even ennoble with the word "style." These villages were transformed by the most basic form of industrial construction seen throughout the poorer countries in Africa, Asia, and South America: a gridded concrete framework is laid, then shoddily filled in with masonry or concrete; the roof of the four- to six-story buildings are left with rebar sticking out of the concrete columns, as if they might be built even higher. A house of this sort can sprout up in just a few days. By the time the authorities catch on, it's already built. And it will remain unfinished; in a place where it so seldom rains, one can do without a decent roof.

Cows, donkeys, and goats have stayed on, as have chickens and ducks. They have moved into these new, multistory houses with their owners, and they all live side by side. The donkeys still carry towering heaps of green fodder that considerably exceed their own size. North Africa is the most plausible present-day setting in which to imagine Apuleius's imperial Roman novel *The Golden Ass*. The story is about a man who is accidentally turned into a donkey and forced to endure the beast of burden's fate; it is close to the mark when it comes to everyday life here.

Muslim and Coptic fellahin, or peasants, still wear the floor-length *jellabiya*, which is no simple sack: these garments are well tailored, narrow at the shoulders and broader toward the bottom – a tunic that gives a dignified silhouette to all kinds of men, trim and portly, young and old alike. Coptic women wear a black dress with tight bodice and wide, calf-length skirt, with a pair of tights underneath; their heads are loosely covered with a black scarf, and adorned by gold earrings. How could people who cling to tradition so firmly, even in their dress, have sped forward with such an unchecked drive to destroy their own environment?

This question met with two stock answers, each of which prompted still other questions. Above all, I was told, this shift was a function of exploding birthrates, a buzzword whose attendant threat of claustrophobia can only really be understood in a country where just 5 percent of the total land mass is habitable. Because the scarce arable land in the Nile Valley is being increasingly developed, agriculturally viable terrain is rapidly vanishing.

The second explanation was that age-old customs of living in extended families had unexpectedly lost traction. As Mohammed had observed in his own village in the Nile Delta, nothing seemed to have changed in terms of family cohesion and the patriarchal order, but all of a sudden, the women of a clan all wanted their own kitchens and no longer wanted to cook together at one communal hearth. This would appear to be the reverse of how development usually works: here, it wasn't wealth stoking individualist desires; these desires developed even where there was no economic basis to support them. There never had been such wealth here, and it seemed highly uncertain whether there ever would be.

The demolition of the old houses did nothing to improve hygienic conditions, incidentally. The streets were still unpaved, and large puddles formed, making the streets muddy as well as dark, since the taller buildings with cantilevered upper stories let no sunlight through. Cow and chicken manure and pools of urine accumulated. In some villages, even in El-Aour, I came upon a once stately structure, the neoclassical townhouse of a noble nineteenth-century family, now abandoned to decay. The canals, which traditionally lined each village, were the saddest sight of all. In a country that is predominantly desert, shouldn't water be treasured?

Instead of water, I saw trash, one of the twentieth century's most diabolical innovations. Even the word is new; you won't find it anywhere in nineteenth-century literature. Sure, there used to be dirt, dung, rubbish, and so on, almost all of it organic. Trash, however, has a different quality. A trash heap, viewed from afar, looks like a mass of white and gray, like the shredded bits of reused paper that pop out of padded envelopes when torn awkwardly. Closer up, this generic pile reveals great diversity: the glitter of aluminum packaging; the delicate mottling of pink, yellow, and light blue plastic bags; black tires; the opalescent accents of plastic bottles, all forming a messy porridge poured into once lovely banks, for miles and miles, turning the water into a dull, toxic broth.

Although such soulless trash is dead, its stench takes on a life of its own. Swarms of truly noble birds, the renowned cattle egrets, have also remained loyal to the new villages. Their long, pointed beaks, curving necks, retractable heads, and raised shoulders remain unchanged, but living on mountains of rubbish has made their once-glorious plumage brown. The filth has swallowed up all their beauty, becoming an inseparable part of their bodies. In eking out a living, they can't really tell the difference between foraging in fields of wheat or poking through trash heaps with their finely curved bills. And humans aren't unlike birds – at the edge of these dumps, men leisurely smoke their water pipes, children play, and a farmer's wife carries a fat duck in her arms as if she were in an idyllic pastoral scene painted by an old Dutch master. Sickly dogs sniff around for food scraps, and little boys, with feet so black they look like they've been rubbed with coal dust, invariably scrounge up something useful as well.

At the same time, modern agriculture has also come to this countryside. The fields surrounding these villages are tilled by tractors, sprayed with chemical fertilizers and pesticides, and look as orderly as the ones in Germany. Here, decline and progress seem to be two sides of the same coin.

In the background, of course, looms the largest watershed event in Egypt's entire history: the construction of the Aswan Dam, which ended the Nile's annual flooding and canceled out the age-old seasonal rhythms. These floods were the source of the country's legendary fertility and ancient wealth. Every year the river submerged the plains on both right and left banks. For weeks entire swaths of land were transformed into lakes, with a wealth of flora and fauna: fish, hippos, crocodiles, water lilies, and ibises. The river then naturally returned to its bed in a cycle resembling the third day of creation in Genesis, the separation of sea and land. The Nile was considered both maternal and paternal: its receding waters helped the fruitful land resurface in a veritable rebirth, and the swiftly moving floodwaters washed away all accumulated debris as well. One can see why, over the course of eons, Egyptians developed an obvious trust in nature's talent for self-purification.

But there is no longer any foundation for such trust. The Aswan Dam's engineers shattered it as they erected the structure and buried entire chapters of Egypt's history under its hulking concrete walls. Has the dam catastrophically damaged the natural habitat of the river's unique landscape? Could harvests have been increased to meet the needs of rising birthrates by some other means? These are now hotly debated topics. But as soon as the mud-saturated, naturally fertilizing waters ceased to ebb and flow, the area's natural rubbish removal also ceased. At the same time, a type of garbage that had never existed before started flooding every city, town, and village – the world had changed, but people and their habits hadn't adapted. Since then, the relationship between farmers and their environment has been ruined. Change came all too suddenly. Such developments have thrown off kilter the harmony handed down from generation to generation, and the possibility of a new harmony has yet to emerge.

Sameh

8

The Martyrs' Houses

SOMEONE WHO AIMS TO ASSESS a foreign culture must listen to its people. Not just what they say, but also how they say it – how they express themselves, what dialect they speak, and their grasp of grammar are all key components in assembling a fairly complete picture. My reliance on interpreters (I don't speak Arabic) was thus a huge obstacle: every day a different young man who spoke scant English introduced himself to me in this role. Each one made the friendliest possible effort to help me converse with the martyrs' family members, but I couldn't help feeling that I must have missed out on a lot. And so, in my quest to learn more about the personalities of the Twenty-One, I also relied heavily on my eyes, scanning their ancestral surroundings for traces of their lives, as if their absence had left a void that could hint at a rough outline of each man's character.

Sadly, my hopes of visiting the homes where they grew up turned out to be in vain. This wasn't because the families wouldn't welcome me, but rather because most of the houses were gone. For although the Egyptian government had basically sat back and watched, without intervening, as the Twenty-One were taken prisoner, it sprang into action after their beheading, which the whole world had been able to watch online. General el-Sisi not only rushed to show his indignation but also to help the martyrs' families. They had lost their breadwinners, but they had gained saints – and just what that meant must have immediately been clear to the head of state. He understood it was time to show his concern.

In the West, from the nineteenth century onward, a special cult of relics has developed around the legacies of major cultural figures. Much as the church continued to enshrine the bones of its saints upon the altar, people began preserving the homes of secular "saints." Goethe's residence in Weimar is probably one of the first. And soon the Catholic Church began imitating the practice as well, here and there – the hovel where Bernadette Soubirous, Seer of Lourdes, lived can still be visited today, for instance, complete with the same kitchen sink and cooking pots she used.

One is at a far remove from any such devotion to documentation and preservation in Upper Egypt. Almost all the houses the martyrs were born and raised in were demolished and replaced by new ones with the help of the state. Just two years after their death, only one of their homes survived. This last one – "the rest were exactly like it," people I spoke to on the streets told me – led me to conclude that most of the others were also old-fashioned adobe brick houses. This means the families of the dead were among the village's poorest; all around them, newer concrete houses had long been popping up. With help from both the church and state, these families had been given what the Twenty-One would have had to labor years to achieve, had they survived.

I stood at the destination of a journey that, back home in Germany, I had imagined being immensely difficult. I thought of the three wise men who had followed a star and were then astonished to find themselves before a stable, yet instantly knew they had come to the right place. No matter which of the martyr's houses I visited, the front door was always open, and children played on the steps. The masonry betrayed the apparent fact that no level had been used in its construction, and the bricks' unevenness was hidden under a washable wallpaper of sorts. The houses did not look rustic but had a more urban appearance – even when the room just off the entryway held two lean cows with dirt-caked undersides and udders, ruminating on fodder as their urine trickled into the forecourt. Even when the houses were brand new, they were traditionally furnished, in a common style that looked like a holdover rescued from otherwise entirely demolished environs.

A lot of new furniture had been bought, but not everything old had been tossed out. Two items in particular always survived the transition: I discovered the same table from the village carpenter in every house, its legs turned on a lathe, and at least one wooden bench with a well-worn back, its seat so deep one can sit fully cross-legged. The throne room of a Near Eastern prince clearly inspired each salon, as living rooms and front rooms are referred to throughout North Africa, because the thrones of sultans, moguls, caliphs, and emirs were traditionally a sofa with thick cushions. In palaces, the sofa that served as throne was surrounded by other sofas, benches, and armchairs lined up along the walls, with small tables in front of them for guests' tea glasses. The magnificence of such a room – gilt furniture, brocade cushions, and precious rugs – was still considered worthy of imitation throughout the country, and for all walks of life: just as vassals gather around their prince, farmers' families gather around their patriarchs. And so, in the homes of the martyrs' families, in the room right next to the cow stall and its related odors, guests were invited to sit on benches lined by thick pillows of dark red velvet embroidered with gold thread. Upon leaving this salon, one found the rest of the house was mostly a shell, a condition the inhabitants seem to have resigned themselves to.

The salon ceiling called for extra effort, and received particular attention. Its white background was adorned with gold stucco crosses and grapevines, common symbols of Christ and Dionysus, reflecting the syncretic beliefs of Christianity's earliest centuries. One of the martyrs, the house painter Luka, was adept at painting various types of trompe-l'oeil marble; his parents' house had been under construction before his death, and he had decorated it. A circular fluorescent light hung from the middle of the ceiling, but the walls were made of gray concrete splattered with the same white that covers the ceiling, as if it were a work of lyrical abstraction. Apparently the construction of these houses followed the same trajectory as those throughout the Egyptian countryside: it began with an inspiring plan, construction was undertaken with determined will, and it all could have been beautiful if the momentum hadn't eventually been lost – if the family hadn't lost interest and abandoned the project. Such houses were destined to enter a phase of decay before even being completed.

This became particularly evident in the four-story house of one of the families' neighbors. Its interior was plastered with vividly patterned tiles, and they had even planned a few large bathrooms. Did the contractor run out of money? In any case, they must have just given up, and the bathrooms and tiled salons became stables for ducks, chickens, turkeys, and pigeons. The birds had proceeded to make the rooms their own, covering the floor with slimy droppings atop a solid crust of guano. It was as if Egypt's very soil was avenging those who trampled its age-old laws by stoking such a clumsy building boom in such fruitful terrain, while failing to accomplish anything healthy or whole.

Apparently a new house had to be half in ruins, and the newly-forged frame rusting, before its inhabitants would fully move in. Back in Cairo, a devout Muslim had told me that the Islamic faith carried an instinctive resistance to any human being's intention to accomplish something perfect, since perfection can only be achieved by God. As a goal of human endeavor, striving for perfection is almost considered blasphemous. It was a nice thought, but could anyone really believe that these villagers regarded such neglect of their surroundings in terms of such a philosophy? The more time I spent in Upper Egypt, the more I began to imagine that this overall, permanent state of structural incompletion wasn't just a testament to people's poverty, but that perhaps something else was behind it. In the end, could it actually be considered something of a style?

The fact that there really was a common sense of style was also visible in how pictures were hung in these rooms: always high up, salon-style, with one frame right next to another, the bottom flush with the wall and the top tilted outward, the way oil paintings are often hung in order to reduce glare. Of course, there were no oil paintings in the martyrs' houses, just prints – some older, some newer, all flyspecked – which proved that the ecclesiastic tradition of icon painting, which wasn't highly developed here anyway, clearly didn't mean much to the village's families: there were baroque Italianate Madonnas, and others that echoed nineteenth-century Russian icons. I saw more than one Jesus portrayed as the "Divine Mercy" described by the Polish saint Maria Faustina Kowalska, with multicolored rays of light, and I also saw several unfamiliar portraits of Jesus with a wavy beard. There were photographs of reigning Pope Tawadros II in full regalia, as well as pictures of the local bishop, and pictures of the family's grandparents, who looked so far removed that they could well have lived in the time of the pharaohs, although most had died at a young age. Even today, many Egyptians never reach old age.

It was in rooms like these, which even in the poorest houses boast a curious solemnity, that I was received both ceremoniously and at the same time rather informally. Sitting opposite me, at a distance, the men got comfortable, stretched their legs out on the bench, leaned into the brocade cushions, and held one of their bare feet with one hand.

The more unfinished the room, the more beautiful it was. When I visited the family of Saint Bishoy, for example, the walls were carelessly painted in a way that resembled a splotchy oil slick. The light coming in the windows was dimmed by pitted and yellowed panes, the purple-and-gold pillows lining the benches shimmered in the dim light, and dots of light on the glass covering the tilted pictures made the images indiscernible. The atmosphere was so thick you could cut it with a knife – rife with tragedies, dreams, and everyday life – and time floated lazily by like the brown currents of the Nile.

In the adjoining room, a dark cave of sorts with an earthen floor, a calf bleated loudly for its mother, drowning out our conversation. In front of the calf stood a pile of fodder so green that even in the dark it looked like a spring meadow. Swallows swooped in and out of the cowshed, where they had built their nests. They spent winters in Egypt and summers in Germany, along the Baltic Sea, effortlessly migrating between the two countries each year. I would have liked to be a swallow, if only to become more familiar with these people.

We drank tea. It was hard to shake the spell the entire scene cast on me. Had the martyrs unexpectedly come home, they would have had the bewildering experience of seeing everything ineffably transformed, yet still the same as ever.

Luka

9

With the Martyrs' Families

MY VISITS WITH THE FAMILIES all followed roughly the same course, but were also a little strained by the fact that I showed up not only with the somewhat sullen pastor, but with a string of young interpreters sent by the bishop. We must have seemed like an envoy complete with entourage, presuming right of entry and approaching each home as if no one dare turn us away. One of the interpreters had studied theology, another had already become a deacon in service of the metropolitan, and still another was the aforementioned pharmacist who worked in Saudi Arabia. There were several others, but the one commonality was that they all lived at a far remove from the realities of everyday village life.

I had asked whether we should confirm our visits with the martyrs' families in advance, especially since I was hoping to meet them at home. I was told that this wasn't necessary, because people are always at home, or at least the women would be. It is considered improper for married women to work outside the home, even to tend their own fields, even if the family is extremely poor. This ancient law seems to have taken on a new significance in these times of unemployment and overpopulation.

The parents, wives, brothers, and sisters of the martyrs were quiet, friendly, confident people. I was coming to them from a country they would never have heard of if it weren't for soccer (Bayern München was a team name that commanded respect here, although that didn't mean anyone was interested in knowing where Munich was or even what Bavaria might be), but I didn't encounter any diffidence, self-consciousness, or excitement. I was welcomed with a dignified, politely reserved distance. In the wake of February 15, 2015, many people had paid them a visit: the head of state and his large retinue; the pope of Alexandria; and all the bishops of Egypt, with entire flocks of monks and priests. Even laypeople made their way to El-Aour. Once the church was consecrated, a steady stream of Coptic pilgrims could be expected – Copts and Sufi Muslims share a habitual passion for pilgrimage and spend several days of the year going to various saints' festivals around the country.

So the martyrs' family members weren't surprised that so many people came to visit. Their husbands, sons, and brothers had experienced the most amazing transformation of all: they had left home as poor migrant workers and would never return, but had become saints and were now more present than ever, albeit in a different form. They now wore crowns, even though they had only done what was expected of them, and what all their brothers were equally prepared to do. Unexpectedly, this natural fulfillment of duty, which would otherwise be taken for granted, was surrounded by the greatest splendor – but this served only to prove that little more than the thinnest veil separates earthly life from the heavenly sphere. One must always be prepared for the possibility that this veil might tear, letting a golden ray of light fall into the realm of everyday life. Precisely by accepting such a cruel fate, their husbands, sons, and brothers had been magnificently exalted. The martyrs' relatives made no pretense of sharing their late loved ones' glory, but they did take calm pride in them.

Sixteen of the Twenty-One had been neighbors in El-Aour and lived on the same village lane. Life there was lived in public, without much privacy, just as it had been in rural Europe at least until World War II, and in many places for a good while after. Contemporary Westerners suffer from not just a general historical amnesia, but a genealogical amnesia as well, and it seems to have erased all knowledge of how their own grandparents and great-grandparents lived. Countries where such living conditions continue into the present day are regarded with condescension and pity, as if they've failed to strive for and reach a prescribed socio-economic goal. The horror such long-preserved ways of life inspire carries with it a particular kind of prudery – as if what is widely termed "backwardness" also implies some kind of moral failure. To be perfectly clear: the Twenty-One never slept on sheets, so had never experienced the physical benefits of a freshly made bed. It's entirely possible that they were well acquainted with fleas and lice; none of them had a bathtub. The fact that their families now live in new houses, and that some of them own a refrigerator, hasn't much affected their way of life. But in each of the living rooms of these homes there is a picture of a murdered son wearing a crown and the white robe of a deacon. Much like King David, who once lived in a shepherd's hut, a king has emerged from each of these families.

All the houses I visited shared one common feature: the household was not in mourning. Condolences and expressions of sympathy seemed out of place. Each family seemed to me to have somehow been elevated to another plane. A scorching flash of violence had struck them, followed by a majestic clap of thunder that had slowly faded yet never fully died out. Now, at the end of the lane on which most of the martyrs had lived stood the massive, bare, concrete dome, looking so foreign that it might as well have been beamed down from outer space.

Language alone could not do justice to the men; certainly, the archdiocese was at a loss when it came to describing their individual personalities for the official martyrology. After all, the available biographical information was sparse.

"He was quick to forgive, argued with no one, and was faithful and honorable" (Magued).

"He served his whole family" (Hany).

"He was friendly and had a kind heart" (Ezzat).

"He slept with the Bible on his chest. He prayed and strictly followed the fast" (Malak).

"His peaceful smile showed how close he was to God" (Luka).

"He gave alms even though he was poor" (Sameh).

"He carefully considered his words before opening his mouth" (Milad).

"He was discreet, respectful, and calm" (Issam).

"He was calm, obedient, and quick to confess" (Youssef).

"He devoted a lot of time to helping the 'Lord's brothers' – the poor" (Bishoy).

"He was a man of prayer and liturgy" (Girgis the younger).

"He was a quiet man, even when criticized" (Mina).

"He was an honest worker and treated his parents with respect" (Kiryollos).

"His heart was pure and simple, his words humble" (Gaber).

"He was compassionate and strove to help others" (Girgis the elder).

The common thread running through all these descriptions is discretion. Pray, serve, stay silent – that's an apt characterization of a monk. But they weren't monks, much as Kiryollos might have wanted to become one. He was the only one said to have had such a wish, but hadn't made the cut – monasteries judged postulants according to strict standards. He met the criterion of being unmarried, but that was only a function of his young age: in the world he came from, remaining celibate without having taken a religious vow wasn't part of the plan. He would have married by the age of thirty at the latest, most likely to a girl from his extended family whom he had known since childhood. In clans that often encompassed up to three hundred families, there were certainly enough prospects.

Couldn't one easily conclude that the episcopal registrar had tried to craft an exemplary past for these new saints by distilling their lives into a sententious formula? After my visits to El-Aour and the neighboring villages, however, I suspect that he simply wrote down what he was told. I heard exactly the same things he had.

"He was good – a good son, a good husband, a good father." These words, repeated to me each and every time, sounded too modest, too ineffectual for men who were now the stuff of legend. It seemed likely that this trait of discretion was a hallmark not only of the twenty-one martyrs, but of the entire region and its villages – a shared heritage not in the sense of stubborn omerta, or enforced silence, but rather of a circumspection that made coexisting in such close quarters for unchanging days, months, years, and decades a little more bearable. In a village where everyone knows everything about everyone else, gossip can make life a living hell. The widow of Tawadros – at forty-six, he was by far the eldest of the martyrs, and had left her with three children – said of her husband, "He was honorable and simple." Might not the Virgin Mary have said the same of Saint Joseph?

The pastor was the only one I heard who gave the matter a different spin: "You have to understand: these were average young men, completely normal guys. I never would have thought they would become saints!" It still perplexed him – if only he had known!

Well, if they were indeed your average young men, then the bar for what was average had been set pretty high.

Tawadros's widow recalled that in Libya he had been told to change his Christian name, Theodore, lest it cause him trouble. His reply: "Anyone who starts changing his name will end up changing his faith."

Just before bidding me goodbye, the widow of Magued – at forty-one, he was the second eldest of the Twenty-One, a coarse-looking peasant with a low brow and dense hair – said with visible embarrassment, as if it were hard for her to confess: "He wanted us all to be angels."

The young widow of twenty-eight-year-old Samuel (the elder) showed me a professional family photo in which she, her husband, and their three children posed before a backdrop featuring a futuristic skyline. She added that whenever her husband called from Libya, he always asked whether the family was praying. It was his last question on every call.

Twenty-six-year-old Milad kept the fast even when working long, hard days in the fields, against the pastor's advice. His reply: "Man does not live by bread alone." That is how I heard it from his widow, who looked to be not much older than a girl, her mourning attire almost costume-like. He had sent her his Bible from Libya, and she always carries it in her pocket. She can't read, but is preserving this precious keepsake for their children.

Twenty-three-year-old Girgis (the elder), newly betrothed to his cousin, would often stay in his room, praying, for two hours. His one-eyed, white-turbaned father pointed out to me its closed door, covered in colorful holy images, as if his son were still behind it. Incidentally, his family still lived in an old adobe house with umber-colored walls, beamed ceilings, and earthen floors. While we talked, sure-flighted swallows darted through the room, and a rat scurried across the adjacent stable.

The young widow of twenty-eight-year-old Luka, who never met his own daughter, recalled how he could read minds, including hers: "He always sent me money, even before I could tell him I needed something." After my visit with her I learned that these young widows would never remarry, solely because they had been married to a martyr.

The mother of the brothers Bishoy and Samuel (the younger), a petite, gaunt woman, held a picture of the latter that portrayed him with the large eyes and gentle face of an icon. He always said, "I am the king's son." When he was twelve years old, a stone had fallen from the third floor and struck his head. "He was in the intensive care unit when the Blessed Virgin appeared to him and said, 'Fear not,' and not long after that he was healed."

The household of twenty-three-year-old Mina has preserved one of his handicrafts – a scale model of a Coptic church as big as a birdcage, with domed towers, arches, and windows lit from inside by a colorful, flashing string of lights. With the exception of the faux-marble decorations painted by Luka, it is the only personal testimony we have that is straight from the hand of one of the dead. According to Mina's mother, he was once miraculously spared serious injury: "The buzz saw slipped and had almost reached his hand when the power unexpectedly went out." She listed the many accidents from which he had been saved, echoing a motif found in the lives of so many martyrs of the past. "As a boy, he survived a serious electric shock; soon after that, he plummeted from a third-story window to the street, but was only slightly injured. In the monastery of Saint Samuel he tumbled, head first, down three hundred and fifty steps; even that didn't kill him." He had overcome many dangers to meet his final destiny.

Only the mother of Kiryollos, who had given birth to five other sons, had nothing to say about her son. A cheerful mood prevailed in her home, and a young uncle who was a priest joined us. Wearing his cassock, he leaned comfortably into the big cushions to tell me about his late relative:

"He never said much, never thought about the future. He just lived one day at a time." Was that what I thought I had read on his face in the video of his execution – his somewhat lost gaze, his slightly absent expression, the look of someone daydreaming? Even once his head was severed, his face had still preserved a touch of that expression.

It had been dangerous to go to Libya seeking work. The Arab Spring had plunged the country into chaos, and public safety was effectively a thing of the past. There had been violence against Christians well before 2015, including several murders. The priests of one Egyptian diocese – the Holy Metropolis of Damanhur, in the Nile Delta, who also looked after the Copts in Libya – ceased their usual trips, as there was no reliable police force left to protect them. But the families of the Twenty-One needed the money, and going to Libya was a shorter journey and posed fewer bureaucratic difficulties than going to the Gulf States. They were poor – just an inconspicuous little group heading out to look for jobs together. Who would care about such people?

And yet their departure was accompanied by a few premonitions. Twenty-three-year-old Abanub, a young man whose unusual features made it look as if he might be from India, said to a friend returning home to El-Aour from Libya in 2014 to get married: "You came back here for your wedding this year, but in 2015 we will all celebrate our wedding." Might his listeners have been reminded of the "marriage supper of the Lamb" from the Book of Revelation, which all of them would have been familiar with, in which the blood of the sacrifice cleanses the robes of the righteous until they are pure white? After the fact, that is precisely how his enigmatic words were interpreted.

Girgis (the elder) was also twenty-three and, according to his father, always carried a photograph of two Christians killed in a bombing, saying: "I wish I were with them, and like them."

Sameh phoned his family shortly before being abducted – he had been in Libya for six months already – and asked not only that everyone back home pray for him, but above all that they look after his little daughter.

Issam's widow showed me a photograph people considered prophetic. During a visit to the Monastery of Saint Samuel, Issam had asked a monk what the future might hold. Issam knelt silently before him, and the monk put his hands around the young man's neck – that was the exact moment the snapshot recorded. On the night the Twenty-One were abducted, the monk had a dream: he saw Issam and other men tormented by a large hound dog in uniform, and then a dagger suddenly pierced his chest.

Luka's widow said that once, after hearing a sermon on martyrdom, her husband had said: "I'm ready." He mentioned having an intuition that martyrdom awaited him. He had often taken walks on the very beach where he was later beheaded. He also had a macabre sense of humor: she showed me a photograph of him lying in a coffin he himself had built. As I left, she gave me a T-shirt with a print of her husband and Issam, both wearing sparkling crowns.

Malak's father, a fat, merry farmer in a gray *jellabiya*, described a phenomenon that occurred the night after the murder: a bright white light appeared in the dark sky, "like a laser cannon." He and the neighbors spotted it even before news of their sons' deaths had reached them. He recalled that, throughout the forty-three days their sons had been held captive, the government had kept all the men's families in the dark, without any news. "We didn't know how they were doing, but as soon as we saw the light, it was clear: either they've been freed, or they're dead." He had begun to join our visits to other families, and let others confirm this miracle as well; and indeed, they, too, had seen it.

Phenomena involving bright lights are a recurring theme in Coptic narratives, and accompany almost all major events the church has experienced over the centuries.

The miracles didn't stop, even after the massacre. The little son of Samuel (the elder) fell to the street from the third floor, and his arm was broken in several places. When he regained consciousness, he claimed his father had caught him, and a few days later his x-rays showed not a single fracture. Samuel's sister, who entered the door barefoot in a stained *jellabiya*, confessed that for three days following the death of her brother she had fought with God: "I blamed God!" But then a bright light had appeared in the heavens, Samuel's face shining brightly from within. "After that, twenty-one crowns appeared around the light. From then on, I didn't complain anymore."

Sameh's son, who fell ill and began vomiting after his father's death, also saw him again: Sameh had laid his hand on the child's head and said, "It's going to be all right," and the boy had immediately felt well again.

Ezzat's mother, a stout woman who had borne seven other children and had a noticeably spirited eloquence compared to most of the people I met here, suffered a severe stroke a while after her son's death. Ezzat and Saint George had come to her in a dream; her son had laid his hands upon her, and she had been healed.

A childless Muslim woman came to Issam's mother for help – local Muslims often ask their Coptic neighbors to pray for them: "Your God listens to prayers and works wonders." She gave the woman one of Issam's shirts. Maybe the woman wore it when she lay with her husband – who knows? In any case, after fifteen infertile years, she became pregnant twice while in possession of the shirt.

The martyrs had often saved children falling out of windows: after his death, Luka, too, had caught his two-year-old nephew, saving him after he fell from the fifth floor.

This served as confirmation – not just for the families, but also for their neighbors and many others in the surrounding countryside – that the martyrs were indeed now with Christ. Their steadfastness had led to their sanctification (this is why they were portrayed wearing crowns) and they now served as mediators of divine grace for their fellow human beings on earth.

All of which is why their families didn't care to remember the grief, pain, and fear they felt during the men's captivity, nor the tears unleashed by the news of their deaths. In fact, they all went out of their way to avoid leaving me with the impression that the decapitation of their sons, brothers, and husbands had caused them any misfortune. Naturally, they were depressed while awaiting news, as they had been kept in the dark and could only prepare for the worst. But when they saw the video and knew with certainty what had happened, their confidence had returned: "We now have a holy martyr in heaven and must rejoice. Nothing can harm us anymore."

This also explains why the families handled the execution video with such apparent ease. There was an iPad in every household where the full-length, uncut, unedited version could be watched. Malak's mother was the only one who refused to look at the screen, while all the young men, cousins, and brothers in the household, as they had often done, stared at it, apparently undisturbed, pointing out the men they recognized. There could have been no better place to watch the video – surrounded by the men's families and runny-nosed children, in rooms adorned with images of the crowned Twenty-One, while a goat poked its devilish-looking head through the doorway and a calf next door wauled for its mother.

What would the murderers say about their video being shown like this? Would it surprise them to see how unflappable these simple-minded, poor folk were; that these people had managed to turn an attempt at triggering boundless terror into something entirely different? Would they be able to see that their cruelty had failed to achieve its intended goal, that their attempt to intimidate and disturb hadn't succeeded?

Gaber's hunched-over, barefoot mother – whose house had resounded with unidentifiable voices singing a hallelujah at the hour of his death, as her Muslim neighbors also confirmed – was quick to express her gratitude that her son had become a martyr. Youssef's family members – his young widow with their little boy, his turban-clad father, his mother holding an icon of her crowned son to her chest – told me, as well as each other, how happy they were when they realized that he was in heaven. Gaber's family had a similar response.

Hany's mother also readily admitted her joy, especially with regard to her four little grandchildren: once they're a bit older, they'll be so proud that their father is a martyr.

Milad's parents also thanked God for their son's martyrdom, and the parents of Girgis (the elder) recalled how their son had always wanted to become a martyr. During his captivity they had not prayed for his deliverance, but only that he remain strong. He had remained strong indeed, and was now the family's pride and joy.

All these words were spoken not with fanaticism or zeal, but rather with serenity and calm. These were no Spartan mothers celebrating some rigid ideal, but believers whose faith had been forged and strengthened by adversity. Whereas Georg Büchner's *Danton's Death* features Thomas Payne asserting that pain is the touchstone of atheism, in this case it turns out to be quite the opposite: pain is the touchstone of faith and the revelation of Christ.

Ezzat's mother, who had been cured of stroke by her son's supernatural intervention, was the only one who still seemed to feel equal cause for both mourning and rejoicing.

As she spoke to me, her lively eyes grew moist. Malak's father, the otherwise cheerful colossus, drew her close and embraced her. He had shown us his son's Bible – he himself was unable to read it, but gave it a reverent kiss before putting it away for safekeeping. He knew many passages by heart, and began quoting from the Second Book of Samuel in the Old Testament, where David inquires about his son.

> "Is the child dead?" They said, "He is dead." Then David arose from the earth and washed and anointed himself and changed his clothes. And he went into the house of the Lord and worshiped. He then went to his own house. And when he asked, they set food before him, and he ate. Then his servants said to him, "What is this thing that you have done? You fasted and wept for the child while he was alive; but when the child died, you arose and ate food." He said, "While the child was still alive, I fasted and wept, for I said, 'Who knows whether the Lord will be gracious to me, that the child may live?' But now he is dead. Why should I fast? Can I bring him back again? I shall go to him, but he will not return to me."

"You understand?" Malak's father continued. "We've done just as King David did, or at least we've tried." But at that he, too, lost his composure.

In the many conversations I had, never once did anyone call for retribution or revenge, nor even for the murderers to be punished. It was as if the families wanted nothing whatsoever to do with them, because the martyrs' sheer splendor outshone them, leaving them to become immaterial *lemures*, as the ancient Romans referred to such spirits – the wandering, formless, vengeful ghosts associated with darkness and condemned to be hunted by Satan for all eternity. The martyrs had "fought the good fight," "finished the race," and "kept the faith," as the apostle Paul writes, in a line all of them would have known well.

Or might this type of surrender be the result of centuries of experience, repeatedly proving that persecution of the Copts never was and never would be penalized? Could turning this inherited defenselessness into a wise refusal to be vengeful constitute a virtue?

I must also mention the reliquaries that can be found in many of the martyrs' houses. The bishop of a neighboring diocese had taken the Pauline notion of Christian life as a race or competition quite literally and given the families polished metal trophies, as if the martyrs were a victorious soccer team. The church had also given them large hardwood reliquary cabinets with three glass doors, decorated with vines and crosses carved by hand. In El-Aour's neighboring villages, these cabinets are less richly decorated and made of utilitarian metal instead of wood, as if destined for a pharmacy, but they also have three doors and are equally large.

The cabinets usually stand in their own small room, an oratory, which houses not only the reliquaries and trophies but everything else the men left behind: shirts and shorts; *jellabiyas* and mobile phones; their liturgical robes; the embroidered white tunics they wore in the church chorus; the cymbals they played during the liturgy; souvenirs of their many pilgrimages; and even the Bibles of those who could read. Their bones hadn't yet been found when I visited, but according to ancient Orthodox tradition even the objects touched by saints are considered venerable relics. The families expected that when the martyrs' remains were transferred to the sanctuary, each family would be given a swatch of the blood-soaked jumpsuits, after which the rest of the garments would be given place of honor in the reliquaries.

The back wall of the cupboard behind the middle door often had a placard with the hymn the Coptic Church had dedicated to these new martyrs – a simple verse that, like a litany, recited all their names and sang their praises. The composer of the multi-stanza hymn had managed to make it both memorable and rhythmic. Before I bid each family farewell, everyone gathered in the salon. Relatives both young and old, as well as my ever-increasing entourage, stood before the reliquary and sang the hymn, their hands raised in prayer. I didn't understand the text, but the repetitive rhythm reminded me of the psalmody that accompanied Sufi dances I had once seen in Cairo's City of the Dead.

To my ears, this type of singing didn't sound particularly sacred, but rather cheery and playful, like a children's counting rhyme. Might there be a spiritual affinity between those sounds and the songs of these God-loving brotherhoods? The hymn didn't resemble the songs of the Coptic liturgy. It seemed to me that its goal was to take each individual's flood of grief and pour it into a single, shared current capable of transforming such sentiments. The tired-out formula we constantly talk about in the West as the "grieving process," which in self-help books gives one an oddly technical take on how to overcome pain, is no theory here: this music allowed one to experience what mourning could really mean. By opening one's mouth in song, loss became reverence, grief became gratitude, despair became joy, and the tune carried everyone away. Once again, I couldn't help but wonder what the killers would think if they were to hear these families singing, hands raised high, before their rough-hewn shrines. Would they hear it as the abominable idolatry of non-believers whose sons they rightly killed? Or, if they were truly devout Muslims, might they be able to glean something more from such singing?

When I later asked myself what I had actually learned about the martyrs during my weeks in El-Aour, I was at a bit of a loss. Understandably, when reworked photo-ID pictures and relatives' stories are the only thing one has to go on, it's not easy to get a fully developed impression of a dead man. Malak was the only one I saw a slightly more personal photograph of: it showed him freshly shaven, his cheeks rosy, in a shiny black jacket, white shirt, and loose tie, striking a little pose. Was his right hand on the knot to further loosen the tie, or to tighten it? He gazed straight at the camera, giving the viewer an expectant or perhaps encouraging look. Was he on his way to a dance party, or a date? Why was the pastor so emphatic about the martyrs being "average young men"? A vast labyrinth spreads out behind the term "average guy." What's "average," anyway? Might this young man be the village Romeo, a brawling soccer fiend, or a hard partier? Did he like to pick fights, or race around on his motorcycle?

I have to admit that these are the kinds of things that come to mind when I hear about an "average guy." Poverty and life in such a tightly-knit extended family might have been like straitjackets of a sort for people here – and the "average young man" indulging his lust for life might have hit a wall sooner here than in the less monolithic cultures of the West – but even in El-Aour the existence of such desire, and people's attempts to pursue it, had to be reckoned with somehow.

Why hadn't I at least carefully ventured in that direction with my questions? I'm not much of a reporter. Professional journalists enjoy a lack of restraint I find hard to muster. I gave myself over to the surroundings and mood I encountered in the homes of the martyrs' families and didn't feel I had the right to disturb them with probing questions. What more could prying inquiries produce, anyway? The beheaded men's new presence as saints and miracle workers was more important to these families than anything in the past.

It was none other than Malak, the young man in that picture wearing the tie (one the photographer had loaned him?), who spoke the decisive words for the Twenty-One. The pastor told me about their last conversation before Malak left for Libya. The pastor had pointed out that believers could bear witness not only by dying for Christ, but also by living a long and faithful life. "That's not enough for me," Malak had answered. "I want to bear witness through death."

Mina

10

Saint Menas's Oil

THE COPTIC CHURCH is officially known as the Egyptian Orthodox Church, but icons, which mean almost as much to Orthodox Russians and Greeks as the consecrated host does to Catholics, do not enjoy the same status here in Egypt. The country was already under Islamic rule during the 150-year bout of iconoclasm that swept outward from Constantinople in the eighth and ninth centuries, so the imperial order to destroy all sacred images would not have reached the Nile Valley. Rather, it appears Egypt had fewer icons to begin with. An iconography of the sort visible in the works preserved at Saint Catherine's Monastery, on the Sinai Peninsula, was nonexistent here. Although it's true that there was a Hellenistic painting tradition here during imperial Roman times – artists who produced the highly realistic, vibrantly colored portraits later rediscovered in the desert sands of the Faiyum Oasis, which survive to this day and are considered by many art historians to be the point of origin for all icons – that tradition was clearly lost long ago in Christian Egypt.

And so it seems that the earliest icons aspired to be nothing more than realistic portraits. Artists were forbidden to portray Jesus and Mary on the basis of their own imagination. Icons constituted an important, highly compelling expression of the Trinitarian religion. If God had become man in the form of his Son, and had thus received a face – unimaginable for the God of the Old Covenant – then it was only logical that the face God showed to the world would be portrayed in paint. Thus, portraying Jesus on an icon was a confession that the incarnation of God is to be understood neither mythically nor spiritually, but rather historically, as an event that really took place. Yet, although Copts still hold to this idea today, even their scholars cannot always explain why this ancient iconic tradition, which became highly developed in Hellenism, never really took off in their church.

And yet we also must not overlook the fact that most of the old churches were destroyed. Monasticism may have begun here in Egypt, but by the nineteenth century there were only five monasteries left in the entire country, and they, too, had been robbed of their libraries and artistic treasures. Given such an obstacle, how could a proper painting tradition develop?

Perhaps the culture of the Mamluk sultanate, with its staunch adherence to the idea that portraying sentient beings in art is tantamount to idolatry, discouraged and intimidated the Copts. One example of this can be seen in the tall wooden wall dividing the sanctuary from the congregation in Coptic churches: unlike the iconostasis or "pictorial wall" present in Greek and Russian churches, Coptic churches have a chancel screen that closely resembles a *maqsurah* in some mosques, often featuring ornate geometric inlays of precious woods and camel bone, but no representational pictures. Painting made a comeback in the seventeenth and eighteenth centuries; Egypt had come under the Ottomans, who also oppressed the Copts but were apparently less arbitrary than the Mamluks. The icons of this period show delicate, pretty, doll-like faces. Jesus and Mary are shown in high-priestly or royal attire, on thrones, surrounded by fields of gold. But these particular icons are usually rather small and don't much resemble the awe-inspiring Greek Orthodox icons – they're more reminiscent of baroque southern European folk art.

Now that so many large new churches are being built, there is an attempt to root contemporary imagery in older traditions: using black outlines and solidly-drawn figures whose heads are then painted in, artists are harkening back to historic illuminated manuscripts. The result is an archaic stylization not unlike the sort visible in modern church art in the West. Egypt's new ecclesiastical paintings often also aim to narratively illustrate biblical scenes. This is an entirely new element in Coptic church art, which previously placed more value on simply portraying saints. The idea was that saints should constitute a *communio sanctorum,* or "communion of saints," surrounding the sacred space.

Thus, photographs of these new saints on the Libyan seashore have played a unique role. The fact that most portraits of them are based on their passport pictures – the least artistic genre of all – naturally makes their images much like traditional iconic portraiture.

These new sacred images are closely tied to the Bible. It's almost as if certain lines from the Book of Revelation were directly related to the Twenty-One: ". . . and I saw the souls of them that were beheaded for the witness of Jesus, and for the word of God, and which had not worshipped the beast, neither his image, neither had received his mark upon their foreheads, or in their hands; and they lived and reigned with Christ a thousand years."

Such visions are fulfilled even where the details don't exactly match up. For example, the original Greek of this Bible passage suggests that the martyrs were beheaded with a battle-axe; in our case, the martyrs' necks were instead severed with knives that the executioners had to laboriously push and pull, back and forth, until the blade

passed through. But many contemporary Egyptians actually do have a mark on their forehead: truly pious Muslims
(as well as hypocritical and hyper-sanctimonious ones)
often have a dark callus on their forehead, which shows
how eagerly they bow to the ground during prayer. Some,
according to my defense lawyer friend Mohammed, even
help things along a bit by abrading their skin when prayer
alone doesn't suffice.

The martyrs, on the other hand, all wore a different
mark: a small Coptic cross tattooed at the base of their
thumb, which was certainly not the "mark of the beast."
Therefore it was only logical, and in full accordance with
scripture, to portray the new saints wearing crowns on
posters and postcards. Why then are they shown wearing
European-style, open-topped royal crowns that look as
if they were lifted straight from some Disney animation,
rather than the enclosed, bulbous crowns worn by patriarchs of the Eastern Orthodox Church? Of course, this is a
question that would only occur to a Westerner.

The Western church also has pictures of crowned
martyrs, but they are all old. These depictions, which take
Revelation at its word, are still appreciated as antiquities,
and art connoisseurs savor how the Van Eyck brothers and
Rogier van der Weyden rendered the ornate gold crowns in
their works. But is there a single bishop today who would
commission a picture of Saint Maximilian Kolbe, for
instance, wearing a crown? Such an idea is unimaginable
even in his native Poland. And yet these crowns simply say,
in drastically unmistakable terms, what the church has
always believed of its saints: that they were Christ-like, and
should therefore be exalted, entering into eternal splendor.

That is why it would be an oversimplification to interpret
the crowns photoshopped over the Twenty-One's passport
photos as a mere sign of societal backwardness, or a vain
attempt at appropriating a long-outmoded signifier of

power. The most recent Egyptian monarchs to wear crowns were the Pharaohs, and theirs looked quite different. Even the very last, highly Europeanized kings of Egypt did not wear crowns like the ones these new martyrs are shown with. These crowned martyrs are about as far removed from political royalty as their role model Jesus Christ, who called himself a king even though his country had had no real royalty for a long time at that point. A strict phenomenologist might come to the conclusion that a Christian church no longer dares represent its saints in crowns for fear that believers might consider it aesthetically appalling or view it as a poor stand-in for the idea of an afterlife – of eternal life. Still, their canonizations do have the air of a posthumous award ceremony, as if the saint were receiving a medal. Most Copts view the issue rather differently.

And yet contemporary photomontages of the new saints are amazingly faithful to tradition. A mid-sixth-century icon from the Coptic Monastery of Saint Apollo, near Antinopolis, portrays Egypt's patron, Saint Menas, who was martyred during the Diocletianic Persecution. His reliquary church and monastery were built on the spot where the camels in his funeral procession knelt down and refused to continue, and it soon became one of the most visited pilgrimage sites of late antiquity. This early icon shows Menas beside Christ; both are the same size, and the only difference between their halos is that Jesus' features a cross. The Savior's arm is around Menas's shoulder, and Christ seems to be pulling Menas toward him, as if they were close friends. Their oversized eyes are reminiscent of the aforementioned Hellenistic Faiyum portraits, and the rest of their bodies are stylized, paying no heed to the laws of anatomy. It's art from a transitional period: the image doesn't have the power of earlier works, yet a new style has yet to emerge. And couldn't one make a case that, more often than not, we apply the term "archaic" to work that, in truth, signals a painstaking attempt at a new beginning after the downfall of a dominant culture?

But it's the gesture that matters here. Across the millennia and many stylistic periods, this expression of physical closeness between Jesus and the saint has lasted into the present day. Contemporary Egyptians who are baptized with Menas as their patron saint have the given name Mina. No wonder the name of a martyr from the church's earliest era also appears in the flock of these new martyrs. Mina, who died at twenty-three, had retained a full, almost childlike face; he stood out among his fellows thanks to his narrow eyes, as if he were of Eurasian descent. One photomontage places his picture right next to that of the Savior: Jesus of Nazareth, apparently clipped from an American-style illustration, leans down toward the passport photo of Mina, places a hand on his cheek and, eyes closed, kisses the crown of his head.

This depiction aims to open believers' eyes to what really happened on the beach of Sirte, by inviting viewers to see through the sheer cruelty of the massacre to grasp the underlying event. In this reading, the massacre itself was just the tip of the iceberg. Copts would consider it a mistake to dwell too long on this superficial, external aspect – even though the families of the dead don't avoid it, as the unedited, uncensored video every household keeps on hand makes clear. But what really matters for them is that the invocation of Jesus' name placed the dying men in the immediate vicinity of God. Circumventing what usually awaits the dead – namely, the last judgment – the martyrs have gone straight into the arms of Christ, who receives them as his equals.

The means used to represent this were somewhat different in the sixth century than in the twenty-first century, although artists of both eras worked in the uncertain period between the end of an established tradition and the beginning of something new and still indefinable. After all, it is already evident that the term "kitsch" – which arose with the advent of modern art at the beginning of the twentieth century and has played such an important role in the dismissal of any and all countermovements since then – is gradually losing its discriminatory power.

Even without the word "kitsch," Goethe touched on the subject in 1790. This was during his second, not entirely voluntary visit to Venice, and he was clearly growing weary of Italy's charms. His aesthetic formulation is more wide-reaching than it might seem at first: "Miracle-working images are usually just bad paintings." Yes, "bad paintings," at least according to the academy's standards, which were all-powerful back when he wrote this. And yet that little "just" also seems to pose a contradiction. Indeed, although the Catholic Church inspired an unprecedented volume of artistic production, none of its leaders ever wondered why the masterpieces it commissioned were never particularly venerated by believers, were never prayed to, and were never closely associated with any actual miracles. Even Raphael, whose Madonnas essentially rose to the rank of Western icons, never painted a single image that worked any miracles or could otherwise be considered miraculous. It's as if the church's simple believers had a subtle, entirely unconscious intuition, a conviction that an image that intended to represent the contemporary era as supernatural couldn't also be associated with some ambitious, aesthetic subjectivity. The anonymity of the painter – who served his sacred function by taking an established visual form and repeating it anew, however awkwardly – was a prerequisite for the holiness attributed to his work, which was thereby considered believably close to the saint it depicted.

It's hardly surprising, then, that even the belabored photomontages of the martyrs created by local photoshop amateurs are not considered miraculous by contemporary

Egyptian Copts, who instead shower attention on a basic passport photo of Mina. It's blown up to a standard letter-sized sheet and might have been artificially colored even before his martyrdom. His lips are a glossy light pink, his eyes black, the skin of his soft, round face white as snow. This picture is kept in his parents' house, and his still youthful mother showed it to me. Something strange had happened to it. It was covered in shiny droplets, a brownish liquid having dripped down its surface from above. It was as if his open, friendly face were sweating. The drops gave his vague smile a baffling expression, as if behind his apparent calm there lurked a deep fear. As his mother explained, these drops were an oil that appeared out of nowhere on the first anniversary of Mina's death, and again on February 15, 2017, for the second time. She collected the oil in little plastic bottles, and gave me one to take home. But the police had forbidden her from making too much of this miracle – they wanted to prevent the masses from descending upon the village and causing unrest.

The grave of Mina's patron, Saint Menas, at the eponymous monastery in Wadi Natrun, also developed such drops. They were collected beginning in the fourth century, and pilgrims who came from all over Europe brought them home in small clay vessels bearing the monastery's seal. So-called Menas bottles have been found as far afield as England. Now that the monastery has been rebuilt, it has recently begun selling them again. And today, once again, Saint Menas's oil – albeit from another saint, the recently martyred Mina – flows from his image as a sign of his supernatural support and physical closeness. Such signs give the Copts courage and fuel their conviction that the church has found a connection to its earlier heyday.

Matthew

11

Matthew the Copt

THE *MARTYROLOGIUM ROMANUM* lists August 30 as the feast of the holy martyrs Felix and Adauctus. Felix was likely a Roman citizen sentenced to death in 303 during the Diocletianic Persecution. En route to his execution he was spotted by an unknown onlooker who, moved by the sight of Felix in chains, professed his own Christian faith on the spot. He was then beheaded alongside Felix and, because his name remained unknown, is worshiped as Saint Adauctus, "the added man."

The Copts martyred on the beach in Libya also had an Adauctus among them – a young black man from Ghana who was abducted along with them. Initially his country of origin was unclear, and during my visit to El-Aour there was still talk that he might be from Chad or Senegal. But given the inaccurate grasp of geography among the people I was with, the mention of these place names likely meant little more than "from far away." There were probably no Copts in his homeland. The kidnappers, I was told, thought he wasn't a Christian and wanted to let him go. But he didn't think it just: whether he was Catholic, Protestant, or belonged to another Christian sect, he didn't much care for such distinctions. And so the kidnappers had to take his word for it; he was a Christian and said so, and that was enough for them to kill him alongside the others.

At first I thought it plausible that the *Synaxarium* called him "Matthew" out of convenience, simply so they didn't have to speak of yet another "Adauctus." In the meantime, however, I've learned that his name actually was Matthew – and he couldn't have been better named in order to become a Coptic saint as a dark-skinned Sub-Saharan African. Matthew the Evangelist and Apostle, who was martyred in Ethiopia, is traditionally credited with founding the Ethiopian Church – the sister church of the Coptic Church founded by Mark the Evangelist. So even though Matthew was not Ethiopian, his name connects him to the Coptic Christians of all Sub-Saharan Africa. The Coptic Church has respected his refusal to be separated from his fellow prisoners, and therefore made him one of its own sons.

The only pictures we have of Matthew are stills from the video that show him kneeling in the sand, among the Egyptians, in an orange jumpsuit. It seems that no one in his homeland missed him for quite some time. While the Egyptians were accompanied on their final journey by the hopes and prayers of their relatives, Matthew's didn't learn of his fate until later. He looks both devoted and resigned; his expression shows no fear or tension whatsoever. His killer holds him by the collar, as if worried that he might jump up and run off at any moment, and so his bare neck, which will soon be severed, is almost completely exposed. His posture is especially straight. He might have understood the threatening speech the killers' leader gave in English. At any rate, he surely had no doubt about the gravity and hopelessness of his situation. But he didn't see that as any reason not to hold his head high. Things could not have been worse, but he seems to have recognized that there was nothing he could do about it.

What kind of man was Matthew? He had ventured from West Africa to the Mediterranean as a migrant worker, and was voluntarily beheaded alongside men from another nation. What conclusions might we draw from the little we know of him?

"I am a Christian," I am told he said – not, "I believe in Christ." Belief belongs to the realm of meaning, certainty, conviction; it is something we declare about ourselves that invariably carries risk, since no one is as unknown to us as ourselves. Often enough we have had the experience of a seemingly absolute certainty, an incontrovertible thought, beginning to inexorably decay as soon as it has been uttered, such that we realize – with a sense of relief as well as a guilty conscience – that we are clearly going to have doubts about what we have just professed. In Mark 9:24, the epileptic child's father commits himself to Jesus with these prayerful words: "Lord, I believe; help my unbelief!" Few people in the surrounding crowd who claim to be believers dare leave after the boy's miraculous return to health.

In contrast, the words "I am a Christian" contain a liberating degree of objectivity. True, Christians become Christians through faith, but there is also an aspect of the sacraments that doesn't depend on faith: one becomes a Christian through baptism. (Christianity also entails the undeniable fact that spiritual transformation can be brought about by means of material things such as water and oil, wine and bread.) A baptized person can also say "I am a Christian" when overwhelmed by doubt because, according to the church's teachings, even the most corrosive doubt cannot alter the efficacy of baptism. But Matthew's declaration, "I am a Christian," leaves no room for doubt or any other such out-of-place considerations. It all must have been quite simple for him.

I imagine his Christianity was as indisputable for him as his skin color. Denying his Christianity, as I see it, would have struck him less as a betrayal, and more as giving in to hopelessness. He likely would have found it pointless.

His captors just hadn't looked closely enough when they
tried to let him go – on closer inspection, they would have
quickly realized he was so sure of his faith that it might as
well have been written on his forehead. The man so calmly
kneeling there in quiet anticipation of the knife that will be
brought to his throat is – one might imagine – not only the
son of another land and civilization, but also of a time that
has long since sunk far down into the darkness of history:
a time in which people knew exactly who they were, and
trusted that language presupposed reality, sealing one's
fate and leaving no doubt about what it rendered. Accounts
of people proclaiming "I am a Christian" when they know
the consequence will be death have a fairytale-like ring
to our contemporary ears. One might be tempted to say
that it is impossible for anyone to think that way today,
had Matthew's blood not flowed from his throat into the
sea at Sirte.

That the Coptic Church counts Matthew among its new
saints was by no means a given, however. Had he survived
and expressed a desire to be accepted as a Copt, he would
have had to be baptized again since, like many Orthodox
churches, the Coptic Church does not recognize baptisms
performed by another church. So is Matthew simply an
unbaptized person who somehow became a saint? Not at all.
By his willingness to die alongside his Coptic companions,
he received the baptism of blood on the Libyan seaside: his
own blood took the place of both the holy water and the
priest's christening.

Issam

12

Abuna Bolla and Abuna Timotheus

WHAT HAPPENED TO THE TWENTY-ONE on February 15, 2015, on the beach of Sirte isn't a distant memory. We have photos of their faces, a video that documents their deaths, and immediate family members who are alive – one would think it would be easier to follow the trails they left behind than those of the historic martyrs, who might have been famous yet didn't always leave much of a trace. Even with luck, the most we can usually uncover about past saints is a mere record of court proceedings, as was the case with the apostles Peter and Paul. Before his own martyrdom during Christianity's early years, Tertullian, a North African lawyer, claimed to have seen Peter and Paul's court records, pointing to the fact that as a constitutional state, ancient Rome did not execute people without due process and documentation. More often, however, there are little more than anecdotes passed down through the ages, and legends that have little to back them up – tales that today are generally considered pious inventions, since they can't withstand rigorous scientific or historical review. Predictably, not a single portrait of the historic martyrs created during their lifetime has ever been unearthed.

Even in the case of the Twenty-One it is difficult to cast light into the darkness that now surrounds their lives, and in the end it may prove impossible. It's as if they have been placed in a quarantine of sorts that prevents anyone from getting too close. As the metropolitan told me, no witnesses saw them during their forty-three-day imprisonment, other than their guards and executioners. And although the killers documented their crime in the video, they were careful to keep their own identities and the events of the preceding period tightly concealed.

My search for the last people to have seen the martyrs before their capture led me to Damanhur, in the Nile Delta. The city is an old episcopal see, but there is nothing about it that would suggest it is any more than thirty years old. During my travels I had already noticed that flies in Egypt have more of a tendency than flies in Europe to gather as a blackish throng, especially wherever sweet tea has been spilled on a coffeehouse table. And these new-old cities of Egypt struck me in much the same way – like a swarm of flies surrounding a decaying carcass. Here again, though, entering the grounds around the cathedral and the epis-copal residence was like stepping into another world: everything was clean and orderly, but also heavily guarded, as had become necessary since the Egyptian revolution so celebrated in the West.

Damanhur is Egypt's largest diocese, and extends far beyond Egyptian soil – it stretches across North Africa, and has become particularly important since Coptic migrant workers have moved to Libya, Tunisia, Algeria, and Morocco. It is from Damanhur that the priests who minister to the spiritual well-being of such laborers set out. Damanhur is also home to the two priests who had been entrusted with the pastoral care of all Copts in Libya, until the disintegration of the Libyan government. Following the overthrow and death of Colonel Gaddafi in October 2011, it was no longer possible for them to continue their work there.

Abuna Bolla and Abuna Timotheus were already connected to each other by name, although the age and relationship between their patrons was the exact opposite of theirs. In English their names would be Father Paul and Father Timothy, respectively. In scripture, Saint Paul was the elder and Saint Timothy his disciple. Here, Bolla was the younger of the two and Timotheus the older, with thick glasses and a long white beard. Both priests had the polite and modest appearance of kindhearted philanthropists: Abuna Bolla with a seemingly permanent smile and gentle wrinkles at the corner of his eyes; Abuna Timotheus's gaze magnified by his glasses, always looking somewhat amazed.

They received me in an office so narrow that their big, baroque armchairs were pushed up against each other, and it almost looked as if one were sitting on the other's lap. Coffee was served immediately – a welcoming gesture of hospitality the conversation couldn't begin without. Abuna Bolla had brought along his daughter, a young woman in jeans who spoke excellent English. The two clergymen's work had never called for any knowledge of English, but Bolla's daughter was preparing for a trip to America. She interpreted almost simultaneously, enriching the priest's words with an added touch – her own verve. Phrases that sounded affectionate, polite, slightly melancholic, and modest coming from the two clergymen gained a fiery enthusiasm through her interpretation. And expressions they seemed to punctuate with a cautious question mark gained an exclamation point; she beamed and laughed while interpreting, as if amused by her own certainties. There was no distance whatsoever in her words, only an exuberant zest for life that drew momentum from the clear joy she took in being a Copt.

At first the priests apologized for having made me wait until Mass was over. Even on weekdays they celebrated several Masses, each lasting three hours. "Our people want it that way; our people love to pray." It almost sounded as though Abuna Bolla felt a need to defend his parishioners' zeal, but his daughter repeated his words with particular enthusiasm, expressing deep love for every unconditional and passionate aspect of their faith, and noting that prayer was a key part of it. A Coptic church must have many altars because, according to canon law, Mass may be celebrated only once a day at any given altar. Since each Mass calls for a different, "fresh" altar, the large new cathedral in Damanhur – like many other large new churches across Egypt – has two levels accommodating two sanctuaries, one right above the other. The one on the ground floor is more modest, while the one above it is the high-vaulted main church. This gives each structure twice as many altars.

I pressed the two men to talk about the martyrs, but my expectations met with minor disappointment: the last time both priests had seen them was several months before the abduction. Before that they had met often, since the workers consistently requested priests' visits. Then it had grown increasingly dangerous for the two to travel to Libya. The Libyan government fell and civil order collapsed. One day a couple of men abducted Abuna Timotheus. Although the young woman clearly wanted to tell me about the incident, his head dropped with embarrassment and his eyes wouldn't leave the floor.

"He doesn't want to talk about that," she said, with an irrepressible, victorious smile. But *she* still did, and though he felt it wasn't important, she insisted, and simply started speaking, first in Arabic and then, after his reluctant nod, in English. "They dragged him into a house."

"Who is 'they'?"

"Men – strangers, Muslims, they didn't say who they were." Once inside, they tore the cross from his neck. It hurt, because it was on a strong leather cord. Then they beat him – for the next four hours.

Father Timotheus squirmed, visibly uncomfortable.

"Then something unexpected happened." Neighbors came, helped him onto the roof terrace, from there onto the neighboring roof, and then down to the street again. "Then he found a taxi and was able to flee to the Egyptian embassy. A miracle," said the young woman.

At this, Father Timotheus joined the conversation again, agreeing with a sudden nod, clearly still amazed and grateful. Wasn't it exactly like Acts, when Peter is liberated from prison? "And, behold, the angel of the Lord came upon him, and a light shined in the prison: and he smote Peter on the side, and raised him up, saying, 'Arise up quickly.' And his chains fell off from his hands." The Bible says nothing about what the angel looked like – in Father Timotheus's case, why shouldn't he have looked like a neighbor?

But such a miracle didn't give them the right to tempt fate with the expectation of divine help a second time. And so, after this liberating yet simultaneously distressing experience, Abuna Timotheus did not return to Libya. After surviving a separate attempted abduction, Abuna Bolla also stopped his westward journeys. His daughter looked at him tenderly as he spoke, for although it might be comforting to be protected and guided by miracles, it was equally good to have her father safe at home.

So the Twenty-One – or rather, the Twenty, since Matthew the Ghanaian had only joined them toward the very end – had remained without an official spiritual attendant for the last half year. Open threats to Christians increased during this time. A Coptic family – father, mother, and young daughter – was murdered, many churches were burned, and others were deserted. But the men from Upper Egypt still didn't return home. Their planned stay had not yet run its course: they had arranged to work ten months in Libya, spend a two-month vacation at home, and then return to work, and their families back in Upper Egypt were counting on the money. Both priests talked about how adamant the men had been about pooling their wages and keeping them safe. They were all staying in a single large room, where they slept side by side on the floor. Not a single piaster was spent for their own enjoyment; everything went to their parents and wives.

After all, in Libya one could earn up to 320 Egyptian pounds a day, the equivalent of about forty-five US dollars before inflation began to balloon, and that was a lot of money. The Libyans were willing to spend on foreign workers, and Libyan nationals were no longer accepting the most basic jobs, so for some time the government had been able to buy a degree of public peace and a fair number of the country's people enjoyed its relative collective wealth. But now all that was over. Safety had become a rare commodity, and soon could not be found at any price. No amount of money can buy something that doesn't exist.

So the men's mistake had been staying in Sirte past the point where it had become too dangerous, I ventured.

"It was no mistake!" the young woman exclaimed. "They knew what was in store for them; they just weren't afraid. They were ready for whatever came their way. We all are!"

And, ultimately, they stood together. Upper Egyptian migrant workers in Libya stuck to the groups they left home in, village by village. They had known each other since early childhood, they had cooked together, and once abroad they had whiled away the hours before bedtime, stretching out, one beside the other, each night.

"No, they didn't while away the hours," the young woman specified while listening to her father, who was intent on giving an accurate portrayal of his former parishioners. "The time they spent together each evening was devoted to nothing but singing, praying, and the Bible – that is, those who were literate read the Bible to the others."

Only now did I learn that some of the martyrs had been illiterate. I had failed to ask about it when I was in El-Aour, out of a foolish sense of shame – I had thought it too embarrassing to delve into, though by then I should have realized that the men's families and fellow villagers were not at all embarrassed. Those who could read didn't have much of an edge on those who couldn't, because they had all already committed the most important things in their lives to memory – the prayers, hymns, litanies, and pericopes pertaining to each part of the liturgical year. And since everyone knew these things by heart, those who could not read deepened their grasp of them while listening to the reader repeat the words aloud.

Indeed, the two priests claimed almost reverentially, the illiterate were precisely the ones nobody could fool. Death had turned the tables: the migrant workers from El-Aour had been more like sons, whereas now the priests looked up to them as the most important people they had yet encountered in their none-too-short lives – people who had bestowed an entirely unexpected meaning upon their own existence. Yes, they had known them and were often asked about them. They had regarded them with love – but the difficulty that now arose was that, back when they went to Libya and celebrated Mass for these migrant workers, they had not had the slightest inkling that these good, pious men – these able and virtuous men, these unpretentious fathers and sons – would later, quite soon, in fact, become what they now were: martyrs. Holy martyrs who wore crowns, who were enthroned in heaven, and before whom the priests whose hands they had once kissed now knelt in prayer.

If only they had looked more closely, back when they still could! The two kindhearted and humble priests had viewed the twenty men not as individuals, but simply as one of the many groups of migrant workers they visited in Libya.

They were all pious, thrifty, and deeply devoted to God and their families. That a supernatural glory now enveloped the men of El-Aour – who could ever have predicted such a thing? Had they even suspected the possibility, of course, both priests would have committed each individual to memory, paying close attention to what distinguished each of them, remembering little incidents and anecdotes. Then they would have had something to tell everyone. Instead, here they were, face-to-face with a visitor who had traveled thousands of miles to ask, expectantly, "What were they like, these holy martyrs?" and they had no good answers at the ready.

"One of them repainted the church in Tripoli." It was the young woman, dutifully interpreting what had just come to Father Timotheus's mind. "But it's gone now – two months after their murder, it was set on fire."

Who was the painter? Maybe Luka, who had done all that fancy faux marble in his parents' house? Or Sameh, who had done decorative stuccos for the salons of his parents' neighbors? Certainly both would have been able to decorate a plain prayer hall and give it a festive look. But the priests had forgotten who had volunteered his free time. It had not been important at the time, and was also a matter of course – it was only natural that the migrant workers happily offered a hand whenever the church needed one.

"They were just there for the church – the church was their second home." It was a plausible answer, and one I heard a lot. Abuna Bolla added that, all in all, Damanhur's bishopric looked after twenty thousand Coptic migrant workers. How could he have picked out individual faces from such a large crowd, even if they were familiar?

But this struck him as too inadequate an answer. He then recalled that the martyrs had turned the large room they all stayed in into a church, since they celebrated Mass so often, said so many prayers, and sang so many hymns.

"Their Muslim neighbors loved them," he added. "Our men were so decent and helpful that they were often called on when help was needed. One cannot simply dismiss Muslims as hostile – regardless of religion, one can still be a good neighbor and express kindness and trust, especially in one's prayer."

Once again, I noticed how the conversation touched upon the willingness of Muslims to ask Christians for their prayers. "They believe our prayers will be answered – in any case, they usually are." The need of both religions for set boundaries is clearly in tension with the need for a sense of shared community – this is part and parcel of the difficult relationship between the two religions. Would German Protestants ever suggest that Catholic prayers were more likely to be answered than their own? Would Jews? For Abuna Bolla and Abuna Timotheus, precisely this experience constituted a not-so-secret triumph, which the young interpreter enjoyed as well – it was as if the Copts held, in the form of their prayers, a supreme weapon that required their enemies to acknowledge its superiority, however reluctantly.

Bolla's daughter proudly showed me the tattoo at the base of her thumb, a little Greek cross which, like a four-leaf clover, had uniform finial ornaments; she had gotten it as a child. Then, with a touch of embarrassment and an apologetic smile, the two priests showed me the crosses tattooed on the back of their hands too. Naturally, they were familiar with the words of the apostle Paul – "May I never boast except in the cross of our Lord" – but their faces betrayed how they struggled with the very concept of "boasting." They would both confess and profess their faith in the cross any time, anywhere, but boasting wasn't really their thing – it suited the young woman much more.

The custom of tattooing a cross on one's hand is quite ancient, she explained to me, and people were doing it as early as the second century after Christ. According to legend, the first instance was when a couple had their young son tattooed with the cross before their own execution, so that he would be recognizable as a Christian when they were gone. When Egypt came under Muslim rule in the seventh century, the custom spread, especially among the poor. "We're proud of the cross; we want to show we are Christians; our faith is strong," the young woman said. Abuna Bolla added that even in Libya, many Muslims now also have a cross tattoo, but on their feet, as protection against scorpion and snake bites. "And of course the recent martyrs were all tattooed too." In other times and places, such distinctive markings had been imposed on members of a minority as part of their persecution, but here it was the minority itself insisting on a distinctive marking that, in troubled times, could become troublesome.

This touched on a question I had been wondering about ever since I learned of the martyrs' fate. Were they murdered because a tide of violence had swept them up with indifference, which is the very hallmark of terror? After all, the theory of *terreur*, as originally formulated during the French Revolution, essentially states that it must be directed against innocents and bystanders as well – the masses are seized by horror only when it becomes clear that neither good behavior nor subjugation nor even assent can guarantee protection. Or did the martyrs actually have a hand in their own deaths, envisioning themselves as being in battle and thus willfully throwing their own lives into the balance?

For the young woman, the answer was clear. "They knew how dangerous Libya was, and they stayed anyway. They weren't afraid of martyrdom – quite the contrary. They were ready to die, and even longed to. We all do! We're all ready and yearning because we all want to vouch for Christ."

It wasn't easy for me to ask about this confession in any greater detail, though I did. She had pronounced it so emphatically that I felt constrained from saying anything that might make it look as if I doubted her words. In light of the video, the fact that the Twenty-One had been killed because they were Christians could not be denied. But wasn't there a difference between being killed merely because one is Christian, and being killed precisely because of one's confession of faith when faced with the threat of death? Wasn't the latter the only instance of true testimony? Traditionally, wasn't choice one of the key criteria for martyrdom? The slain could either cling to their creed and die for it, or give in to their fear of death, deny their faith, and live. In other words, did anyone know whether the Twenty-One could have saved themselves by denying their faith? To put it yet another way, did anyone know if they had been murdered merely *because of* their Christian affiliation, or if they had explicitly been beheaded *for* Christ? There is a difference, isn't there? The thirty Copts who had been assaulted and then murdered in their own homes by their Muslim neighbors in an Upper Egyptian village back in the 1990s had not been given the choice of either reaffirming or denying their religion. Had it been the same for the martyrs on the beach of Sirte, or was there something more to it? Had they manifestly resisted the temptation to fall away from their faith to save their own necks?

The young woman understood immediately what I was getting at, even as the priests shook their heads with uncertainty. She saw that this touched upon an important point. No, it was clear to her: they had resisted – they had been beaten daily, but had not given in. Every evening, after being tortured all day, they had sung together, and all had been as one. And they had repeatedly been offered immediate freedom from their imprisonment and from the looming threat of death if only they would repeat the concise Muslim creed: "There is no god but Allah, and Muhammad is his prophet," *lā 'ilāha 'illā llāh mu ammadun rasūlu llāh.* In Arabic, the verse sounds magically and playfully poetic. And in this case, it could have saved lives.

But how did she know? With the exception of their as-yet-unidentified killers, wasn't there a complete lack of witnesses who could attest to what had gone on during their forty-three-day imprisonment? She said there actually was a witness, although she couldn't put me in touch with him. One of the guards, she said, had admired the prisoners' steadfastness, unanimity, faith, and prayers. He was so deeply moved by them that he had become a Christian. But, again: how did she know? This man couldn't have told a soul without putting himself in immense danger.

The young woman had an answer to that too. He'd had access to the martyrs' mobile phones, and had called their family members and told them. Then he went into hiding and disappeared. He had apparently managed to escape the killers, who would naturally have punished him severely for converting.

An important witness, unfortunately unavailable to answer any other questions – did that disqualify him from offering an assessment of the events, in whatever way possible? More importantly, this question would only have come up had his testimony been in any way contrary to what people generally assumed was already known about the case. Everything led back to the images from the video: the kneeling men's quiet devotion, the absence of any resistance or plea for mercy, the soft calls of *"Ya Rabbi Yassou!"* as the knives cut into their throats. I didn't feel like playing the part of a detective who might have pointed out that none of the martyrs' relatives in Upper Egypt had mentioned any such phone conversations. These people's thoughts and ideas were so focused on the supernatural order of things – into which the events of February 15, 2015, clearly fit – that prodding them to delve any further into factual details was, as soon as I met them, something I felt to be fundamentally off-limits.

But there was one more thing I still wanted to ask: the Twenty-One – whether bachelors, husbands, or fathers – could not possibly have all accepted the threat of such a cruel, imminent death with the same serenity, could they? Each of them, despite all similarities, had his own person- ality. The fact that in their last moments they all showed admirable bravery did not exclude the possibility that one or another had previously expressed fear and doubt. There must have been one who held the group together, who gave them courage and fostered unity so that they could each strengthen the others.

Yes – this was a point all three agreed on – there had been such a man, and the priests remembered him. Our conversation had inspired them and evoked latent images from the past. During their encounters with the martyrs, one stood out from the rest for his willpower and influence over the others: Issam, one of the few who were not from El-Aour, and also one of the few who were not related to the others through extended family. His name wasn't conspic- uously Christian; a Muslim could also be called Issam. At twenty-four, he was one of the youngest, and wasn't married yet, so there wasn't anyone but his widowed mother waiting for him back home. In the video, I had noticed him as one of the two who moved – he was the one who turns his head to his neighbor, Matthew, during the leader's speech, and seems to calmly say a few inaudible words to him. A goodbye, maybe? Or did he think Matthew needed some words of support? Maybe he just needed to fulfill his role one final time, encouraging his fellows to keep up their strength and steadfastness? In profile, he had an aquiline nose; he was fair-skinned and looked as if he could have been of European descent. Might the influence he was said to have had on others come precisely from this – the fact that he looked like a foreigner, and thus somehow stood apart from them?

The priests were reluctant to dwell too long on the possibility of Saint Issam's special role. Seeing the Twenty-One sleep on the floor, one beside the other, for months on end, as a community, they had always viewed them as a group. For Abuna Bolla and Abuna Timotheus, the men had been a choir from which individual voices could not be distinguished – they "heard as it were the voice of a great multitude, and as the voice of many waters, and as the voice of mighty thunderings, saying . . . the marriage of the Lamb is come."

Abuna Bolla quoted these words from Revelation, placing the violent end to the lives of these migrant workers into the only light he felt appropriate, far from the world of contemporary politics and history. On the whole, he felt it essential to stick to the basics, without which, he said, every detail discussed, moving as it may be, meant nothing whatsoever. "Every Christian must have a cross – a real one and a symbolic one, and both must be present. Every Christian must live the life of Jesus anew. Christians in Egypt have always understood this, and that is why Christianity is so strong in Egypt."

The softly smiling man spoke with a touch of embarrassment, as though he felt obliged to make this admonition but was, in his imperfection, not truly entitled to do so. The cheerfulness with which his daughter interpreted his words gave one the impression that there was nothing easier to bear, nothing lighter to carry, than a cross.

As a parting gift Abuna Bolla gave me a soft, round loaf of bread from the Mass they had just celebrated. It was one of the loaves kept on the altar after transubstantiation, and one of the few approved for consumption even by those who don't take communion. This beautiful bread must have had some small flaw, some imperfection – otherwise it wouldn't have been excluded at the beginning of the liturgy, after careful examination, from use as an offering.

Girgis (the elder)

13

The Martyrs' Liturgy

THE OLD PARISH CHURCH OF EL-AOUR cannot be seen from the street, as is often the case in Egypt. It is hidden by a high wall with an imposing gate, in an area where upper-class villagers used to live. The once-dignified homes with their nineteenth-century architecture now lie in ruins, their owners having long since emigrated to Australia or Argentina. Right next to the gate leading to the church courtyard is a watchtower of the sort that has been built all over the country: a concrete pillar about three yards high with a cabin on top, similar to the type of cell inhabited by early Christian pillar-saints. A peasant boy with a shaved head, dressed in uniform, holds an old-fashioned gun out the window as he stands guard. Even here, in a village virtually forgotten until February 15, 2015, a village in which half the population is Christian, the church needs to be protected.

This church is particularly important to me because it is where most of the martyrs were baptized, by total immersion, and where they spent much of their lives. In Egypt as well as in Europe, membership in a church choir attests to one's special commitment to service and community. But among Copts the choir does more than simply embellish the liturgy; it serves a much weightier role. Almost the entire Coptic liturgy is sung; the few spoken parts are whispered by the priest and remain inaudible to parishioners. Even the readings are sung. Because singing is such an essential part of the liturgy, the members of the choir are effectively liturgists. They do not have the same rank as a priest or deacon, but are nevertheless part of the priesthood. They wear liturgical clothing, a white embroidered tunic with red silk sash crossing both their chest and back, and stand on the parishioners' side of the partitioning wall that separates the sanctuary from the pews. Flanking the sacred door from which the priest emerges when he turns to address the worshipers, they stand much like guards. And since the priest's robe is essentially indistinguishable from the choir's tunics – in imitation of the white robes of the elders surrounding the altar and divine throne in Revelation – at a distance he looks much like a chorister. Only his headpiece, a low miter with long white veil extending over his back, sets him apart from his cohorts.

For Copts, being in the church choir means singing for almost three hours straight – no instrumental music, no melodies written by ecclesiastical composers, just ancient chorales and the prayers of the liturgy. The chorales are difficult to memorize, because though the individual melodies differ, they do so only slightly. Indeed, it is a unique type of singing that seeks to fuse the entire liturgy into a single flowing river. And unlike its Latin counterpart, which is made up of distinctly separate prayers, this musical rite is a closed circuit, so to speak, that doesn't build toward a climax but rather begins with one.

Those who want to learn more about the Twenty-One must necessarily study the Coptic liturgy, as it alone constituted the most important mental and aesthetic influence on their lives. They were raised and shaped by it, far more than they were by their few years of school, for those who went to school at all. Six of the Twenty-One were choir members ordained by the bishop – a level of consecration in and of itself – while the others only occasionally sang along. But they all knew the liturgy by heart, since all attended Mass each Sunday and participated in the many customary feast days and other festivities.

One cannot compare the high degree of communalism in Egyptian village life with the everyday circumstances and conditions of city life – after all, lifestyles are not entirely monolithic throughout the country. And in El-Aour, the Coptic families constitute a community whose cohesiveness is constantly reinforced by intramarriage. Within the walls of this church and its courtyard, many extended families come together. Sunday school – a rather recent institution that greatly contributed to the re-emergence of the Coptic Church in the twentieth century – is the only place that provides certain intellectual stimulus.

Within the broader village, the well-kempt churchyard is a domain of unparalleled cleanliness and order. It surrounds a modest church built in the 1960s; it is quite rare to find a church any older than that in a country that has experienced as many waves of cultural destruction as Egypt has over the millennia. Although the Coptic Church's roots date back to the early Christian era, nearly all its physical church structures date back no farther than the twentieth century, and many of those are about to be replaced by larger, more splendid ones.

Even the old church of El-Aour, where the martyrs had been baptized, is little more than an unadorned concrete hall with a choir. Chandeliers with a few missing lights and crystals, images of Jesus of Nazareth in the aforementioned American style, worn-out red carpets, and the red velvet curtains of the *hurus* separating the sanctuary from the pews – like elsewhere in Egypt, this one was made of embroidered velvet wrapped in a shiny protective plastic cover – are the only elements imbuing the space within the otherwise bare walls with a hint of sanctity.

Time and time again I marveled at what an effect such a partition between congregation and sanctuary has. It makes it clear that, even in the most modest of spaces, the church rises, as it were, above the boundary between the supernatural and the terrestrial, between the sacred and the profane. The rite celebrated behind this divider consists of many prayers, but on the whole it aims to be less a prayer than a presentation of the hereafter, a realization of the beyond which intersects with the material world through Jesus' sacrifice. The idea that eternity is present – albeit only rarely experienced – in every moment of a life subject to the passage of time is made manifest in the form of these red curtains wrapped in glittering plastic. It's a point that can be understood visually, without further explanation.

Incidentally, it's worth noting that in Egypt people's relationship to plastic wrap is rather different than in the West. In Muslim households one often finds surahs from the Koran embroidered in gold and laminated in transparent plastic, even when displayed in fancy frames, like a reverential veil protecting the sacred words. Copts, meanwhile, traditionally kiss the red curtains that hide the altar from their eyes, paying no heed to the plastic. Watching this, I realized that although theirs is a piety bound to many, indeed innumerable, outward signs and gestures, it is at the same time completely independent of them.

I often stopped in at this church between my visits to the martyrs' families, even when Mass wasn't being held. I watched the young people who entered the nave every now and then, went up to the barrier surrounding the altar, knelt down to the floor and, after a short prayer, kissed the hem of the curtain. I could picture the Twenty-One doing the same – they had until recently worshiped on this same consecrated ground and received the Eucharist in remembrance of Christ's sacrifice – barefoot, in long gray *jellabiya* or in jeans and T-shirt.

I tried to estimate how many hours of their short lives had been spent observing the liturgy. They were raised on this rite and were absorbed in devotion to a degree that, in the Western world, is often no longer possible even for monks. In a village like El-Aour, this rite unfolded without having to compete with other distractions. Working, spending time with neighbors and relatives, eating, sleeping, and living everyday life in close quarters – it was a life of set habits whose only shining moments occurred in the liturgy.

Life in an Upper Egyptian village left no room for impatience or restlessness. Although TVs were on in the background here as anywhere else, I had the impression that people basically ignored them. There was a colorful, bright, slightly distracting movement on the screen in my peripheral vision – usually their TVs were tuned in to broadcasts from the Coptic Church, the Pope of Alexandria giving an audience, or bishops, or liturgies broadcast from Cairo – but, as in other Mediterranean countries, television was little more than another guest in the house, one given only occasional attention before the host's eyes soon slipped from the screen back to the real world. It seemed to me that the villagers perceived the disembodied nature of images on TV more clearly than most people: its weightlessness and fleetingness stood in sharp contrast to the physical presence of familiar people, the animals in the adjacent room, and the heat, which rose to 120 degrees in the summer and paralyzed even those who had grown up used to it. Or are people who devote such a significant portion of their free time to religious worship simply less susceptible to the virtual allure of the screen?

Indeed, the term *liturgy*, from the Greek roots *litos* and *ergos*, could be translated as "public service" – a parallel of *theurgy*, from the Greek roots *theos* and *ergos*, or "divine service," as the liturgy is often referred to in the Orthodox world. The great liturgies of the Christian world seek to carry out a service for the church: to awaken an awareness of the presence of God, who is the highest reality for those who believe – and even for those who do not, since, logically speaking, atheism can only be defined as doubt in God's existence.

Of course, the Twenty-One never thought in such theological terms, and it is entirely possible they couldn't even conceive of atheism. But even those who had not been ordained were liturgists in body and soul. This has to do with the peculiarity of the Coptic liturgy, whose key moments fully involve the laity. Pope Benedict XVI has called the Latin liturgy "a festival of faith," but compared to the Western tradition the Coptic liturgy is a festival of faith in its utmost form.

Once again – this is impossible to overstate – in order to get to know the martyrs of El-Aour, one must pay close attention to their liturgy, all the more so since its sheer otherness and ancientness make it so distinct from the standard liturgies of the West. Those who celebrate the Roman Catholic liturgy will always have to wonder whether, in its updated form, it still does justice to its apostolic beginnings. Copts have no such reason to wonder, since theirs has been preserved fully intact.

Nowadays when people speak of "the Copts," they usually mean Egyptian Christians, as opposed to Egyptian Muslims. This is a narrow use of the term, which largely corresponds to fact, but it also overlooks the important point that Copts are not primarily a religious community, but a people – the people of Egypt who, alongside Greeks, stood up to the Islamic conquest in the wake of the Pharaohs' rule. The ancient Coptic language developed under Hellenistic rule but was essentially the language of the Pharaohs, and to this day it is used in the liturgy. In other words, the Pharaohs' language lives on in the Coptic liturgy, if nowhere else. The liturgy also grew to include Greek, the language of the New Testament and the Septuagint, the Ptolemaic translation of the Old Testament written in Alexandria. In the second millennium AD, Arabic also became a liturgical language, especially for the reading of scripture, so the Coptic liturgy is sung in three languages. One might therefore say, without exaggeration, that the whole history of the country is present in this service.

When it comes to sacred languages, contemporary Westerners are prone to pose the ironic question of whether the believers even understand what they are singing and praying. It is entirely probable that the Twenty-One would not have been able to translate what they were saying with any precision, but they were certainly familiar with the overall context. An understanding of the details aside, the rite as a whole was, for them, a matter of flesh and blood. The priests who had celebrated the liturgy for them in Libya confirmed this.

Within this context, it is meaningful to note that it was the laity who insisted on keeping to Greek and ancient Coptic when, following the Roman Catholic Church's abolition of Latin, the Coptic episcopacy considered similar reforms. Common prayer serves not only to communicate information, but also provides – and is, in and of itself – poetry, rhythm, and sound. Much as sacred music does, it opens the soul to the divine mystery. And, first and foremost, the Coptic liturgy aims to be a celebration of divine mystery rather than a religious education; the latter is reserved for Sunday school, which takes place after the rite.

Those accustomed to the rite of the Roman Catholic Church will encounter in the Coptic Church a completely different understanding of the Eucharist. The liturgical rite of the West is divided into two major parts. It begins with the liturgy of the Word, which corresponds structurally to the Jewish synagogue service with readings of scripture and preaching. This part – historically called the "Liturgy of the Catechumens," because people who had yet to be baptized were allowed to participate in it – is not considered of equal importance to the following liturgy of the Eucharist. This is why, according to ancient custom, it was unnecessary for all believers to attend the first part in order to fulfill their duties each Sunday – those who attended the liturgy of the Eucharist, with the transubstantiation of bread and wine, had celebrated a fully valid Mass. Although many modern liturgists no longer agree with this assessment, the tradition remains strong: the division of the Mass into less sacred and more sacred portions, respectively, was reasserted in Pope Paul VI's liturgical reform, which largely reproduced the traditional form while at the same time opening it up to improvisation. Now the liturgy of the Word often contains scant ritual elements and includes more talking, instructing, opining, and speeches written by the celebrant.

Any such development would be impossible in the Coptic Church. Although it, too, has discussed potential reforms, the conversations have been limited to topics like reducing the two hundred fast days or slightly shortening the liturgy. The Coptic liturgy is not divided into two parts. From the very first moment, it is clear that the exclusive intention of the holy devotion is the realization of God's presence, and everything that happens in this liturgy has to serve this extraordinary purpose. Here it is clear that, during the second millennium, the cultural differences dividing Rome from Alexandria and Constantinople led the Western liturgy to develop in its own distinct way.

The Roman Catholic Church has made the transubstan-tiation of bread and wine into the body and blood of the Lord the canonical prayer at the heart of the Mass. The words with which Jesus instituted the sacrament of the

Eucharist in the upper room on the first Maundy Thursday, "This is my body . . . this is my blood," are understood as a consecratory formula that triggers the transubstantiation. This has a legal basis: in civil law, spoken formulas have the power to establish or confer a new legal status; in many places the "I do" that spouses utter before the municipal registrar, and not a written vow, constitutes the official step of marriage. Of course, the Roman Church is heir to the ancient Roman state; no wonder, then, that vestiges of its admirable logic remain embedded within this celebration of divine mystery.

The Eastern liturgy and its particular apostolic dignity are a different matter altogether. The consecration of the bread and wine, or transubstantiation, is a long process; it begins with the first moments of the Mass, continues through the entire liturgy, and reaches its climax when, Copts believe, an actual change occurs in the wine and bread as the celebrant utters the Words of Institution and invokes the Holy Spirit.

The opening rite is undeniably impressive. The priest is brought a large basket full of round loaves baked the night before. He begins by carefully examining each and every one; he compares them, returns them to the basket, and finally takes back out the loaf he has settled on as being the most perfect and flawless of all. This loaf alone is destined to be transformed into the body of Christ. The rest of the loaves are later held over the altar, blessed, and then distributed to the congregation after Mass. They play no further part in the transubstantiation of the chosen loaf.

The priest now anoints the chosen bread with water and wine in a motion that makes it look as if he has a piece of soap in his hands, "washing" it like a newborn child, and then wrapping it in a white linen cloth. He holds this bundle in front of his forehead and carries it around the altar, a passage called "the procession of the Lamb." The priest, who here represents the elderly Simeon in the Temple, takes the young Jesus in his arms, and bids his own terrestrial life farewell, "for my eyes have seen salvation." The very act of selecting the bread has already changed this loaf; it is now the "Lamb," and the very act of referring to the bread as the Lamb indicates that the celebrants have entered another temporal realm. "The Lamb" also evokes the great feast described at the conclusion of Revelation, celebrated at the end of all time, in eternity, the aforementioned "marriage supper of the Lamb." And so everyone on earth who celebrates Mass joins in this eternal moment. Time and eternity are bound together as one, in a sphere where past, present, and future have always already happened, and at the same time are now happening again.

The portion of Mass following this "offertory" is situated within the great act of sacrifice; all prayers and readings are subordinated and related to it and structured in such a way that they cannot possibly be misunderstood. In general, the rite aims to maintain a steady level throughout the entire and quite lengthy observance of the Mass. Over and over again, the priest and church members assure and reassure themselves of their faith. The Credo is repeated and recapitulated several times, and the conscious act of offering this sacrificial ceremony – for the entire church as well as for each individual person – is expressed in ever-differing enumerations, as if this public celebration must not exclude a single soul. The destiny of the entire human race – from the Fall down to the present, and through the unforeseeable future – is brought before the throne of God. And since Jesus' death on the cross is considered the redemption of the whole world, this portion also constitutes the realization of his death, a point that must be emphasized. The particularly thought-provoking prayer expressed here is "for all those whom we have forgotten."

The readings themselves also have peculiarities that strongly distinguish them from most Western practice, especially the present-day rite. One of the more noticeable aspects is that the readings are not limited to the Bible. To this day, the Coptic Church remains convinced that Christianity is not a "book religion." Rather, it sees the Bible as only one of the many significant parts of a tradition that entails other commitments and responsibilities as well. Therefore, in addition to the letters of Paul, the second reading – or, more accurately, singing – is from the Church Fathers, the third reading includes excerpts from the Acts of the Apostles, and the fourth is drawn from the *Synaxarium*, the Coptic martyrology and chronicle of the lives of saints. The Church Fathers symbolize the ongoing help of the Holy Spirit, the Book of Acts refers to the foundation of the church hierarchy and casts contemporary bishops as successors to the apostles, and references to the saints render visible the continuity of Jesus within his church. A pericope from the Gospels concludes the readings.

Westerners may well be stunned to learn that the priest doesn't listen to the readings recited by the deacon, but instead spends the time uttering his own inaudible prayers, which underlie the central readings like a prayer rug. These readings are not understood primarily as teaching or preaching. Rather, they serve solely and fully to support the faithful's visualization, evoking the presence of Jesus, the Holy Spirit, and the saints, and must therefore be accompanied by prayer and worship.

The prayer spoken as incense is placed into the censer with a glowing coal is also worthy of mention here. After the prayer, the lectionaries are enveloped in incense: "The golden censer is the Holy Virgin, the scent rising from it is our Savior. She gave birth to him; he saved us and forgave our sins." With this incense the readings are completely enveloped in Christ, as his presence grows ever more all-encompassing, comprising more than can ever be said, either by or about him.

And since the Coptic Church had already separated from the rest of Christendom long before the Greek and Latin churches separated from one another, it has preserved the authentic form of the Credo (as formulated in Constantinople under Emperor Theodosius) whereby the Holy Spirit "proceedeth from the Father," as phrased in the Gospel of John. The papal addition of the controversial *filioque* – which implied that the Holy Spirit proceeded not only "from the Father" but also "from the Son," and led to the Great Schism between Rome and Constantinople – was never even discussed in Egypt.

Now the prepared offerings are revealed. The priest lifts the cloth under which they were hidden and covers his own hands with it. Arms outstretched, he now stands in front of the altar completely veiled, representing the angels of John's apocalyptic vision who, completely hidden under their own wings, surround God's throne.

The "Anaphora" – called the "Canon Missae" in the West – now begins, with a call from the deacon, which is repeated several times over the course of the rite and sounds highly alien to Western ears: "Stand in fear and trembling! Look to the east!" Such words would be deemed "out of place" in the West – for Copts, on the other hand, the contemporary Western concept of the "responsible Christian" who negotiates "eye-to-eye" with Jesus would most certainly be out of place, and probably even seem like a sign of mental derangement. The call to look eastward with the priest stems from the liturgical tradition of awaiting the Lord's return from the east; that is, the realization of Jesus' presence at the altar both anticipates the Second Coming and at the same time announces it.

The moment of actual change is nigh. Roman Catholics can discover a great deal about their own rite from the dialogue between Coptic priest and congregation: the Greek counterparts of the "Sursum Corda" and "Sanctus" can be found here. But the Copts place even greater emphasis – as do the Russians and Greeks, in comparison to the Western church – on the approaching passages, which are experienced as an act of faith. Despite this ancient church's hierarchical conception of a consecrated priesthood, the laity is so deeply involved in the mystery of transubstantiation that the only accurate way to describe it is as a cooperation between priest and congregation. What the priest says and does is constantly confirmed and approved by the congregants. The major reforms of the Second Vatican Council, which resulted in the Mass of Pope Paul VI, included discussion of a *participatio actuosa* on the part of believers – and just what such "active participation" of the laity in apostolic tradition looks like can be experienced through the unchanging rite of the Coptic Church.

An excerpt from the Coptic responsory may clarify this. Imagine the congregation answering the priest with decisively spoken words. Sometimes the celebrants' voices grow tempestuous and impassioned, and the words are chanted or even shouted out.

PRIEST: He has instituted the great mystery and sacrament of his divinity for us, destined as he was to sacrifice himself so that the world may live.

CONGREGATION: We believe!

PRIEST: He took the bread in his holy, immaculate, venerable, and life-giving hands . . .

CONGREGATION: We believe this is true. Amen!

PRIEST: He looked toward heaven to you, O God, who are his Father and Lord of all creation, and expressed his thanks . . .

CONGREGATION: Amen!

PRIEST: He blessed it . . .

CONGREGATION: Amen!

PRIEST: He sanctified it . . .

CONGREGATION: Amen. We believe, we confess, we praise!

PRIEST: He broke it, gave it to his holy disciples and apostles, and said, "Take, eat: this is my body, which is broken for you for the remission of sins. Do this in remembrance of me."

CONGREGATION: This is true! Amen.

PRIEST: Likewise, he took the chalice, after they had eaten, mingling wine and water in it, and expressed his thanks . . .

CONGREGATION: Amen!

PRIEST: He blessed it . . .

CONGREGATION: Amen!

PRIEST: And he sanctified it . . .

CONGREGATION: Amen! Again: We believe, we confess, and we praise!

PRIEST: He took a sip and then gave it to his holy disciples and apostles, saying, "Drink of it, all of you: this is my blood of the new testament, which is shed for you and for many, for the remission of sins. Do this in remembrance of me."

CONGREGATION: This, too, is true! Amen.

PRIEST: Every time you eat of this bread and drink from this cup, you proclaim my death, confess my resurrection, and remember me until I come again.

CONGREGATION: Amen! Amen! Amen! We announce your death, O Lord! We acknowledge your holy resurrection and ascension! We praise you, we praise you, and we thank you, O Lord, our God!

This part of the liturgy is sung in Greek. Although the relationship between the Church of Constantinople and the Church of Alexandria was always strained, the debt Egyptian Christianity owes to the Ptolemaic culture of Alexandria has not been forgotten. As an aside, the Coptic Church learned nothing, regrettably, from its hierarchical struggle against the supremacy of the Church of Constantinople, and later treated its own subordinate, the Orthodox Church of Ethiopia, just as patronizingly.

Shortly before communion, the essence of this liturgy as an act of faith is again made particularly clear as the priest stands before the offering and sings.

PRIEST: The holy body and precious blood of Jesus Christ, Son of God. Amen.

CONGREGATION: Amen!

PRIEST: The holy and precious body and true blood of Jesus Christ, Son of our God. Amen.

CONGREGATION: Amen!

PRIEST: The body and blood of Emmanuel, our God, that is the truth. Amen.

CONGREGATION: Amen. I believe!

PRIEST: Amen. Amen. I believe, I believe, I believe! And I confess, to my very last breath, that this is the life-giving body of your only begotten Son, our Lord, God, and Savior, Jesus Christ, whom he received from our Lady, Mistress of us all, Blessed Mary, Mother of God. He made himself one with his divinity, without mixing humanity and divinity, without one affecting the other, and without altering the two. . . . Truly, I believe that his divinity parted not from his humanity for a single moment nor for the blink of an eye. . . . I believe, I believe, I believe that this is so in truth.

The Roman Catholic Church also believes in the essential transformation of bread and wine in the Eucharist, yet in a much more abstract, idealized form – the explicit mention of Jesus' human physicality, in all its materiality, which is then equated with the materiality of bread and wine, is unique to the Copts. Herein lies the core basis for the veneration of Mary, for which the Latin and Greek churches have their Egyptian brethren to thank. For, unlike the Western liturgy, the Coptic liturgy is decidedly Marian: the Eucharist is an act of incarnation, and the incarnation of God in Jesus came about only because he was born of a human mother. Whenever one thinks of Jesus' human body, his mother must not be forgotten; and the clearer this insight regarding the incarnated character of the Eucharist, the more necessary an emphasis on Mary's part in the process.

Now that the priest and congregation have once again made a strong and clear commitment to their belief in the incarnation, the moment of communion comes. Here, Copts recall one of the most important portions of the Old Testament: the encounter between Moses and the burning bush in Sinai – once again, on Egyptian soil. It is recounted in Exodus 3:2–6:

> And the angel of the Lord appeared unto him in a flame of fire out of the midst of a bush: and he looked, and, behold, the bush burned with fire, and the bush was not consumed. . . . And when the Lord saw that he turned aside to see, God called unto him out of the midst of the bush, and said . . . "Draw not nigh hither: put off thy shoes from off thy feet, for the place whereon thou standest is holy ground." . . . And Moses hid his face; for he was afraid to look upon God.

The new burning bush is the Eucharistic Christ, who, although consumed by so many, is constantly renewed through the liturgy. Thus everyone takes off their shoes before approaching the altar, and the women follow the example of Moses by covering their hair with a veil. Communion, as is customary in this ancient church, is taken by mouth, in both forms, one after the other: the faithful go to the priest, bend their knees, and let a small piece of the consecrated bread be placed on their tongue; they then hold a white cloth over their mouth, as if what they've just received requires close protection until fully swallowed, and then sip the consecrated wine from a goblet held by another priest or deacon. In addition to the clergyman who distributes the communion, there is also a deacon who makes sure no crumbs are lost. If, in spite of his watchful eye, even a single crumb falls to the ground, this deacon goes over to it, kneels down, and picks it up directly with his tongue and lips.

The final hymn is a highlight of the choral sequence. A buzzing sound, which only gradually becomes audible alongside the powerful male voices, mingles with the singing, as if a steel string had been struck – the sound comes from small silver cymbals of the sort mentioned in the Psalms, which accompanied the songs sung in the Temple of Jerusalem. The delicate metallic resonance mixes with the song like a subtle spice that remains hardly detectible in the main course even as it shapes the entire meal. It is almost as if the liturgy had changed the acoustic conditions in such a way that you feel as if you are only now, for the first time ever, truly able to hear. The priest then fills his hands and showers the congregation with holy water: those who are up close get wet; those who are farther back reach their hands up to at least catch a few drops.

This is a highly condensed summary of the rite to which the Twenty-One devoted so much of their energies. And however little or much there is to be learned about them, they can in any case certainly be called *homines liturgi,* men of the liturgy, which in the Western world is now a very rare mode of being human. *Homo liturgus* has left enormous traces, not unlike dinosaur skeletons, in Europe – certain French cathedrals are just one example. But without the associated rite, it is hard to see how such a place of worship could ever have been called a *locus terribilis,* the kind of "awe-inspiring place" one gets a glimpse of reading Exodus. Even when, for instance, prerecorded Gregorian chants play faintly in the background for visiting tourists, it feels like little more than a weak attempt at spreading a vague veneer of consecration. Because of their history of oppression, the Copts have no such cathedrals. And although their ancient churches were destroyed long ago, the columns and Corinthian capitals of those venerable ruins have been visibly incorporated into Cairo's most beautiful mosques.

So they have preserved the rite, because it can be celebrated in all its fullness even in the poorest, most primitive places. It has been preserved in isolation, perhaps precisely so that it can be present at a time like ours, in which Western Christianity appears ready to renounce all ties to its roots in the ancient church. Western critics of the traditional rite often accuse "liturgical men" of exaggerating the liturgy's importance, holding it up as an aestheticism while at the same time neglecting the other pillars of the church: *diakonia*, serving the poor; and *martyria*, bearing witness to one's faith. The Copts don't need their liturgy to be held up as such an example – indeed, for them, the opposite is true: *liturgia* and *martyria* are obviously and inseparably connected.

But I must resist the temptation to idealize the effect this rite had on the Twenty-One. When I visited their village and heard, over and over again, that "they were like all of us," it seems I was to understand that they were not spiritual geniuses, masters of meditation, or extraordinarily gifted men focused solely on the hereafter. The habit – not to say routine – of the liturgy may occasionally have had a lulling effect; perhaps they didn't always rise to the spiritual heights of the rite. In a sense, the rite was the air they breathed, and air is something those of us whom it is keeping alive only really think about when it is absent.

And yet such a foregone conclusion is the precise prerequisite of all ritual. A rite aims to become second nature. It is best when performed with a kind of heightened detachment. Their fellow villagers undoubtedly favored just such a relation to the rite, but when it came to the Twenty-One there was another layer – they were a special kind of community. Back in Damanhur, Abuna Bolla and Abuna Timotheus had called them a choir, and they had been a choir in the most literal sense, singing together countless times, both in the singular position of cantors and as part of the congregation. Western liturgy also speaks of the "choir of martyrs." During their lifetimes, the Twenty-One had already prepared to join this choir.

Abanub

14

The Flight into Egypt

CHRISTIANS IN THE MIDDLE EAST live where the history of salvation recounted in the Old and New Testaments took place. Egyptian Christians have also had to accept that their homeland plays a predominantly negative role in the Bible. The country's glorious ruler – and, if it really was Ramses II, then one of the greatest of all pharaohs – was a bitter enemy of the Israelites. Long after he purportedly drowned in the Red Sea, he remained the evil nemesis par excellence. The liberation of the people of Israel from slavery in Egypt, on the other hand, became a sign of the everlasting assistance God grants his chosen people. For, in the midst of evil, good things happen through God's divine acts of providence – such as the Egyptian ruler's daughter rescuing the infant Moses from the Nile. And it was also on Egyptian soil that, the night before the Israelites fled enslavement, the holiest Jewish feast, Passover, began; later converted and reinterpreted, it became the prototype upon which the holy Mass of Catholic and Orthodox Christians was founded. A church as strongly rooted in its liturgy as the Coptic Church must find such connections particularly significant.

Above all, Jesus himself spent time in Egypt. As Matthew the Evangelist describes it, immediately after the magi presented gold, frankincense, and myrrh to the Holy

Family, Joseph – Jesus' foster father – dreamed of an angel directing him:

> "Arise, and take the young child and his mother, and flee into Egypt, and be thou there until I bring thee word: for Herod will seek the young child to destroy him." When he arose, he took the young child and his mother by night, and departed into Egypt, and was there until the death of Herod, that it might be fulfilled which was spoken of the Lord by the prophet, saying, "Out of Egypt have I called my son."

The idea that Jesus was brought to Egypt as a child is by no means as improbable as most contemporary Western European biblical scholars assert; indeed, many such scholars consider the entirety of Jesus' childhood as recorded in the Gospels of Matthew and Luke to be mere legend. But Egypt was a Roman province and bordered on the Kingdom of Judea, which was governed by the rich Herod on the Romans' behalf. Those seeking to escape his realm had to go from the south of Judea to Egypt, where there were centuries-old Jewish communities. In the ancient Roman fortress called Babylon, in Old Cairo, there are still several synagogues; it was here that the Holy Family apparently took shelter. By the early Christian era, part of the old city walls had already been transformed into a small crypt with ancient columns, and it has since become one of the most important holy sites in the entire country.

Young Jesus spent time on Egyptian soil – this idea has powerfully inspired the Copts' imagination, giving them the feeling that they have a uniquely close relationship to their Savior and the events of his life. Wasn't his flight into Egypt already prefigured by the salvation of the infant Moses? Moses, too, had been in mortal danger when a godless ruler issued an order that the firstborn sons of all the Jews be killed, just as Herod later ordered the death of Bethlehem's firstborn Jewish sons. And by fleeing this death sentence, it is entirely possible that Jesus quite literally took his first steps in Egypt, that Egyptian water bathed him and Egyptian bread nourished him. Egyptians who believe in Jesus feel particularly favored by this story, which they feel confirms their status as chosen ones permitted to follow their divine master down the path of suffering.

Traditionally, Egyptian Christians had an insatiable desire to see their Savior's presence at work not only in the Nile Delta, but across the whole country. Some of the earliest testimonies describe a lengthy journey the Holy Family supposedly undertook throughout all Egypt, at least setting foot in every reasonably important place. To this day many of the Holy Family's resting places are labeled and worshiped as such – the "Rest on the Flight into Egypt," an evocative subject of so many noteworthy Western paintings, could well have been devised in Egypt itself. Anywhere and everywhere the Holy Family arrived, it seems, miraculous signs appeared as evidence that the spot had some connection to this family traveling with only the bare necessities and headed by a humble carpenter. Images of pagan gods shattered or fell, springs sprouted up in previously barren rock, fruits sprouted in the desert, and the sick became healthy.

Back in El-Aour, when I asked whether there were any particular places that were especially important to the Twenty-One, the deacon accompanying me said: "Above all, you have to go to Gebel-el-teir." This rock face on the other bank of the Nile was visible from El-Aour, and looked as if it were floating above the entire landscape. Of all the monasteries and other sacred places the Twenty-One frequently visited, the church atop this rock face was their favorite. Happily for them, it was also close; thanks to its proximity, Copts in the diocese of Samalut regarded themselves as the Holy Family's favored children. A bridge had recently been built over the wide river to connect the two places, making the visit easier than before, when pilgrims had to find a ferryman to make the crossing.

I had found souvenirs from pilgrimages to Gebel-el-teir – little pictures and small plastic models of the church – in all the reliquaries of El-Aour. Every Coptic church has been repeatedly robbed over the centuries, but no one could make off with Gebel-el-teir's greatest treasure: a mysterious imprint left in the rock by the hand of young Jesus. Although their own hands wouldn't fit into it, the martyrs and their families frequently made their way across the Nile to admire this imprint, especially on Marian feast days.

The church itself dates back to late antiquity, and overhangs the cave where the Holy Family took shelter. Its tall pillars have well-preserved Corinthian capitals, and the pillars supporting the small dome are so thick that one of them contains a baptismal font – a Coptic baptismal font, of course, in which the baptized person can be completely submerged. Surrounding the church is a plethora of small tombs stacked together like a cubist composition – clearly, many believers choose to await the resurrection of the dead in this special spot, close to the presence of the Holy Family.

The height of all these pilgrimages is August 15, which is also the highest Marian feast day in the West, when hundreds of thousands of Egyptians come from all over the country to Gebel-el-teir. Peasants from the nearby villages are always among the crowds and are particularly proud to be so close to home, when others have had to travel from far and wide.

The flight into Egypt contained a special secret – the miracle of concealment: despite all the wonders that accompanied the Holy Family's journey, no one was ever able to guess the identity of the child in the arms of his young mother. After all, Jesus was not yet a mighty orator casting a spell over thousands and inspiring individuals to leave everything behind and follow him. He couldn't even talk yet, though in retrospect, his divinity was even more vividly expressed in this mute state of infancy than in his teachings, which may or may not have been uttered or altered by others. To his contemporaries, the most novel aspect of Jesus wasn't his doctrine but his very existence – his flesh, a divine creature incarnate, who moved among both mortals and his own kind.

Speaking of concealment, and of gods and mortals, art historians like to point out that the depiction of the Mother of God with the infant Jesus in her lap, which first appeared in third-century Egypt, is perfectly in place amid the long succession of statues of Isis holding the infant Horus in her lap. Doesn't it only seem natural that such idols easily lent themselves to becoming vessels for new Christian content?

It ought to be noted here that Egyptians, in particular, understood this incarnation of God the creator, who put on the materiality of his own creation, as the true message of Christianity early on, long before there were any sacred images. The belief that God himself became a human infant was a point Egyptians passionately fought over in early Christian times. First came belief in a divine child; the images of Isis and Horus that prefigured Mary and Jesus followed from it, not vice versa, as the aforementioned art historians suggest. In the fourth century this belief sparked conflict between Athanasius the Great, Patriarch of Alexandria, and the Arians, who considered Jesus the creation of God, distinct from the Father. Because he staunchly refused to deny Jesus' divinity, Athanasius was repeatedly exiled, called to trial, and ultimately condemned by the majority of the Roman Empire's bishops and even the pope.

This struggle for official recognition of Jesus' divinity greatly shaped the Coptic Church. It became the church's destiny and to this very day determines the fate of its faithful. Thus the Twenty-One frequently heard sermons on martyrdom emphasizing that it was the Copts who, with all their power and devotion, fought the heathen as well as other Gentiles and Christians to defend Jesus' divine nature.

Athanasius was ultimately victorious, but this, too, had its price. At the Council of Ephesus in 431, the Egyptians managed to depose Nestorius, Patriarch of Constantinople, enabling these Coptic children of the Holy Family to bestow on Mary, Mother of Jesus, the honorary title of *Theotokos*, "Mother of God," and once again confirm their belief in the divine incarnation for the entire church. Yet at the next council – the Council of Chalcedon, held in Asia Minor in the year 451 – the debate not only continued, but culminated in catastrophe: this subtle controversy about the nature of Jesus, which was only exacerbated by linguistic misunderstandings, led to a schism.

For the majority of bishops from both East and West, Jesus embodied two separate natures – divine and human. The Egyptians couldn't imagine such a thing, and insisted that Jesus' divinity and humanity were united in a single, indivisible nature. This view would have been dangerous for the Christian faith if the Egyptians had asserted that because of this fusion of divine and human, Jesus did not actually suffer death on the cross and therefore could not redeem the world. But that was out of the question, as Egyptians did believe Jesus had died on the cross. The quarrel was highly theoretical and barely comprehensible, but at the same time all too understandable: it came down to a power struggle between Constantinople and Alexandria. The Egyptians didn't want to subject themselves to Greek rule, and in the end the Greek and Latin churches – who were in the majority – didn't hesitate to expel the Egyptian church as a whole.

Therefore, the Coptic Church has gone its own way since the fifth century AD; the subsequent Islamic conquest of the country further prevented any rapprochement with the West. In the twentieth century – no less than fifteen hundred years later; it is said churches live in eternity – the dispute over these concepts was settled at long last. The Roman and Alexandrian Popes met and confirmed their agreement regarding the nature of Jesus Christ. Nevertheless, the two churches remain separate, since the Coptic Church still has no intention of being subject to Rome.

Seen from the spiritual point of view, this schism was obviously lamentable. Another result was that the Copts were abandoned by the West and, under Islamic rule, had to carry the burden of oppression on their own. And yet, seen with twenty-twenty hindsight, the Copts' lonely path is nevertheless a gift to the world and all Christendom. In its seclusion, the Coptic Church has preserved the characteristics of early Christianity; no one should say too much about early Christianity without first getting to know the Copts. What the Roman Catholic Church has both gained and lost again over centuries of ongoing development – the exciting story of its rise and fall – pales in comparison to the Copts, who have remained basically unchanged and have always kept the starting point of the Christian religion in their sights.

This short excursion into ecclesiastical history hopefully makes clear why the Twenty-One, as heirs to such a weighty past, remained unconditionally true to their faith. In their isolation, the Copts of Upper Egypt experience the events of the early church as if they had only happened yesterday, and this helps them preserve the simple core of the Christian message. In the beginning was a young woman – really a girl still, just fifteen years old – with a baby not yet a year old, sitting sidesaddle atop a prancing donkey led by her husband, a migrant worker named Joseph. As a group, they looked like so many others, and families like theirs can still be seen today amid the fields around El-Aour. These three souls sparked a change destined to touch the entire world – a change not even the boldest philosophers and scholars of their day could ever have foreseen.

Girgis (the younger)

15

Hierarchical Style

A YOUNG, ENTHUSIASTIC CHURCH – what else could it be, one might wonder, since more than half of Egypt's population is under the age of twenty-five? And this youthful majority has not turned away from the church; instead, it chooses to belong, with deep loyalty and determination. On weekday afternoons in several villages, over and over again, I found groups of young people in the local churches, where they met – girls on the right, boys on the left – to pray together, unaccompanied by the priest. When older people wax enthusiastic about the zeal of the young, it is usually embarrassing. And yet it's worth considering just what kind of church it is that is capable of creating such a sense of belonging among its young adherents – or at least manages not to hinder it.

In the West, youth is often equated with an incomprehension of tradition, habitual irreverence, disregard for hierarchy and rank, and a lack of good manners and respect. The Catholic Church strives, with moderate success, to rise to such challenges. Although it perceives itself as hierarchical, it often deploys a democratic language and style in order to obscure the fact that it isn't subject to democratic conventions. It seems to feel that if it were to convey a sense of its hierarchy, it wouldn't stand a chance with the younger generation, and yet it cannot fully shake its true nature, which remains the same despite the new democratic disguise. Might this dichotomy be what makes the Catholic Church's appeals to young people sound somewhat tone deaf?

Those accustomed to seeing priests in sweaters or shirts and ties, priests eager to blur the lines between themselves and the laity, encounter an entirely different world in Coptic Egypt. A priest without priestly attire is unimaginable here. This garb includes a black cassock; a large cross pendant – a plain cross, not a crucifix – on a braided, black and white leather cord; and a round, brimless, black felt hat. Monks and bishops wear a black cap embroidered with white crosses that ties under the chin, and over it the bishops wear a finely pleated, turban-like black silk hat. A long beard, of course, completes the picture and is such an essential element of a priest's appearance that people joke that facial hair is the sole reason the movement to let women be priests – an idea that has gained such popularity in the West – is not only doomed to fail in Egypt, but would never even cross people's minds. Even outside of church and scheduled Mass, bishops lean on a long crosier with a silver or ivory pommel. In their other hand they hold a cross, which they rarely set down. It is inconceivable that there would be any occasion in which all this could be dispensed with, for priests have neither a private life nor the right to take an evening off.

Wherever and whenever a priest makes an appearance, he becomes the immediate focal point for signs of reverence received from all sides. His close connection to the mysteries of the altar is omnipresent in the consciousness of the laity. People rush over to him, whether they are acquainted with him or not, touch the ground before him with their right hand – a gesture that hints at bowing down while at the same time replaces a full prostration – and then kiss his hand; if he is holding a cross, they first kiss the cross, then his hand. This is the formal salutation everyone adheres to, regardless of station, from childhood to old age. (Sometimes a priest quickly pulls his hand away after someone has already gripped it, as if to prevent him or her from kissing it, but this gesture is a sign of impatience or disfavor rather than modesty. Having at least touched the priest's hand, the lay person might then kiss his or her own fingertips.)

Quite often a priest was born and raised in the village where he is now a pastor, so people have known him from an early age, and have many experiences and habits in common. He has eaten the same bean soup and onions as his congregation on the more than two hundred fast days of the Coptic Church. These austere meals are served by his wife, who sits down only once her husband and his chaplain have finished eating; she then eats what is left over.

Shared origins and experiences do not, however, detract from the reverence shown to priests. In Galilee Jesus said that a prophet will not be recognized as such in his hometown – but that has never been the case for priests in the Coptic villages of Upper Egypt. Upon ordination, the peasant boy becomes a liturgist and mystagogue who, behind the *hurus*, hidden from the eyes of his congregation, celebrates the sacred mysteries. As a messenger from the beyond, his status calls for unconditional respect. When laypeople kiss his hand, they do so with deep joy, as if they consider the opportunity a gift – they might not say so, but you can see it in their smiling faces. Again and again I had the impression that Copts are proud of their priests, bishops, and monks. Further, they seem to perform the striking gestures of submission by which they greet their hierarchs with a sense that they are doing something that is good for themselves too.

Coptic bishops are princes; they emanate strength and dignity. This is a phenomenon that has become unimaginable in the European and American West, where even the most belligerent leaders have to make gestures of humility and modesty before their voters. Western leaders can decide the fates of entire peoples, but must camouflage their power, as democratic protocol demands. It is as if Westerners only tolerate a major power when it disguises itself as a minor one.

But there is something else that, in the Western world, has been wiped out even more thoroughly than the aptitude for respect: authority. In Coptic Egypt, authority takes many shapes. Here one can still grasp the distinction between power and authority, the age-old struggle between the profane ruler and the sacred prophet, between King Herod and John the Baptist. In contrast to Islam, the Coptic Church is strictly separated from the secular state, and therefore enjoys no special protections or privileges. Its status is akin to that of an association governed by private law, with the exception of issues pertaining to family law, which is governed by the rules of the Coptic Church. So in reality, the Pope of Alexandria and his bishops are supported solely by this sense of authority.

All this makes the Copts' tendency to revere their priests more understandable: their bows and prostrations are a source of self-respect. Their priests represent laws over which the state, in its unfriendly neutrality toward Christians, has no influence. The state is powerless to oppose their church's hierarchical order. As seen from the outside, and by many Muslims, the Coptic Church and all Copts are subordinates: their long oppression has rendered them second-class citizens, of dubious integrity and almost contemptible. Outside their own communities, they are often said to be dirty, and people are warned not to eat bread from Coptic bakers.

Seen from the inside, through the eyes of a believer, the Coptic Church is a kingdom full of splendor and mystery, with a hierarchical order that resembles that of the angels and archangels. Whenever they can, the Copts try to pay as little heed to the Muslim world as possible – and the respect they show their priests struck me as a demonstration of the right order of earthly relations.

It may have been mere chance or luck – the sojourner's serendipity – that I happened to primarily meet Coptic bishops who, both externally and internally, convincingly embodied the princely dignity befitting their rank. They were tall and towered above the crowd of their faithful; they had big heads and large eyes like those seen on Faiyum mummy portraits, with prominent noses and long, dense, shapely white beards. When they sat, their heavy bellies rested between their knees, surrounded by the soft folds of their generous cassocks. They resembled ancient Roman river gods, and would make apt allegorical figures of the bountiful Nile overflowing its banks and making the land fruitful.

I also met strict ascetics. There was the bishop in his newly built palace, but there was also the bishop who lived on an isolated desert farm. He looked after girls who had been raped and were sent away to survive the consequences in a complex whose spartan simplicity was much like a kibbutz. This is not to say the latter bishop was any more popular with the faithful, even if the others seemed less committed to the ideal of pious poverty. The splendor in which some bishops live helps poorer Copts, who have no other representatives in a predominantly Muslim society, to hold their heads high.

At the same time, the episcopate is so firmly rooted in liturgy that it isn't measured by secular standards anyway. It would be unthinkable for a bishop to resign, retire, or take the professorial title "emeritus." The idea that believers would look on silently or even approvingly as the press hounds their bishop for some wrongdoing or impropriety is met with complete disbelief among Copts. Such a thing is utterly implausible. To them, as long as he is able to bless, a Coptic bishop performs his episcopal duties in a completely satisfactory manner. And when he is no longer able to carry out such gestures, then his body alone, like an icon of Christ, bestows blessings on all who look upon it.

In Wadi Natrun, one of the recently expanded ancient monasteries, I was informed that an extremely elderly bishop would be making an appearance. A small door opened, and on the threshold stood an incredibly old man with an absent, dreamy gaze. He stood straight, unbowed by age, and still held his crosier and cross, but clearly already resided in another world. Could he still feel the faithful's lips kissing the backs of his hands? His gesture of blessing was implied – after all, he must have at least sensed the presence of the people around him. He had never been more of a bishop than he was now, for he now served strictly as a vessel for a higher will.

Magued

16

A Pilgrimage to the Cloisters

MONKS ARE THE PRIDE of Coptic Egypt. They were the first to recognize the problem posed to Christianity after Emperor Constantine's conversion. The church had just endured one of the worst persecutions in the history of the Roman Empire: at the beginning of the fourth century, under Emperor Diocletian, on some days hundreds of people were executed in Egypt alone. The underlying reasons for this murderous frenzy have never been fully resolved. Was it some kind of persecutory delusion that overcame an otherwise reasonable emperor when he discovered that Christians had advanced to high court offices all around him? Was it a desperate attempt to keep the empire intact, unifying its people by leveraging the binding forces of fear and a cultish worship of the emperor? At any rate, by the end of the massacre, Diocletian had to admit that rash violence had failed: Christianity had gained too many followers and was too well-organized to be so easily exterminated. Although there are no reliable figures, some historians estimate that at this point nearly half the population of the Roman Empire was Christian.

Then, in 325, hardly twenty years later, when Constantine convened the First Council of Nicaea, bishops who had recently been released from imprisonment in Sicilian quarries came bearing the scars of torture on their bodies.

They had now risen to a rank similar to that of the imperial prefects, and found themselves quite literally transformed from hunted criminals to official government representatives. Although in some respects Emperor Constantine's reign was one of the rare periods of true tolerance in ancient Rome – Christianity was as respected as the traditional Greco-Roman religion, and its adherents were no longer subjected to coercion – Christians would soon be put to the test in a way no one was prepared for.

For three hundred years Christian congregations had experienced alternating periods of persecution and tolerance. There had even been periods of semi-official self-determination, during which an extensive network of dioceses formed, but Christians had never truly been treated as equals, and were always regarded with suspicion. Now, all of a sudden, it looked like being Christian might be an advantage. Being baptized opened the door to career advancement, created useful connections, and no longer excluded one from accessing public culture. On the contrary, it facilitated it. And yet there was a particularly ugly aspect of this liberation: the persecuted became persecutors, with history's newest victors treating history's latest vanquished with the same intolerance they had so recently suffered.

During this time, many Christians understood that the church was losing sight of a core ideal: living in imitation of Christ. They had grown up in communities that had witnessed the persecution and killing of fellow believers, and remembered the dead with passion and pride. Perhaps Egypt's Christians had held to their faith more doggedly than Christians in other regions of the Roman Empire, mindful that one must always be prepared to lay down one's own life to bear witness to the faith. But now this need to bear witness no longer seemed necessary – it had become superfluous. And so, for more and more Christians, a key element of Christianity was lost. This new tolerance exacted a high price indeed.

The "great city of Alexandria," as it is still called in Coptic liturgical texts, was one of the most magnificent and richest cities of the Roman Empire. Even though it was technically no more than a provincial capital in an empire whose political centers lay elsewhere, it was nevertheless a citadel of pagan culture where a refined syncretism of Hellenistic and ancient Egyptian religions had developed. Christians here faced the somewhat unique challenge of no longer living as a persecuted minority, turning their backs on the prevailing paganism; they now needed to coexist alongside and amid it. They had to learn to withstand the temptations of pagan culture and engage in intellectual battle with it.

One need only imagine the glamor of ancient Alexandria to understand how its Christians feared losing what they had so heroically preserved through the dark years under Diocletian and before. In this new era Christians were permitted to hold high office and had close relationships with pagans. Little wonder that the great words of Jesus – "He who loves his life will lose it," "Sell all that you have, give it to the poor, and follow me," "Take up your cross," "Those of you who do not give up everything you have cannot be my disciples," "Unless a kernel of wheat falls to the ground and dies, it remains only a single seed. But if it dies, it produces many seeds," and so many others – now sounded foreign.

Nowhere else did cultural opulence so abruptly meet a vast, relatively deserted, and sterile terrain as it did in Egypt, where the narrow strip of arable land on either side of the Nile was so closely and sharply bordered by desert. Those deserts were where the pharaohs had built the tombs that became their impressive legacy. Where human life could not be sustained, the realm of the dead began, and in that realm these richly equipped tombs allowed the pharaohs to continue an existence still partially connected to the land of the living, while their souls had already gone off to face judgment.

But now, after thousands of years, the pharaohs' kingdom had finally faded. Their graves were robbed, the desert was left to Bedouins and wild animals, and living and traveling there had grown dangerous. The first men and women to settle in the desert as hermits wanted to preserve, as their sole and truest inheritance, the defense-lessness their forebears had experienced during periods of persecution. On the western side of the Nile near the ancient capital of Thebes, where barren mountainsides had been excavated to construct tombs for kings, queens, noblemen, and artisans, the first monks moved into the long-deserted caves of the necropolis. It was close enough that fertile land was still accessible, but the infernal heat, freezing cold, and lack of water made life there prohibitive for most. The monks moved into the former tunnel tombs, whose floors were covered in sand and dung, and carved crosses into the delicate bas-reliefs illustrating the deeds of rulers who had died a thousand years before – scenes of hunting and sacrifice, as well as domestic scenes of a highly developed civilization. These shafts invariably ended with a mysterious, eternally closed false door, its coffer carved from a massive monolith – a threshold that could be passed only by the spirits of the dead. After fleeing the worldly city to take refuge in these desert tombs, the hermits now knelt before these false doors, the physical indicators of how far one could venture on earth. Here they would wait until the portals opened.

This region of graves was named Thebais, after the former royal city of Thebes on the opposite bank of the Nile. It was here that the monks' rejection of culture and their refusal to participate in bourgeois doings and dealings, philosophy, and literature created a new culture that would later greatly impact the history of Christianity in both East and West.

A second settlement, Wadi Natrun, sprang up closer to ancient Memphis in Lower Egypt. This particularly inhospitable area lay far below sea level and was once the main mineral source of the natron used in mummification. It is also where the first monasteries came into existence, when it became clear that the hermitages, which had since grown into veritable colonies, needed greater order to help unite their conflicting goals. Here, the faithful could lead the life of a hermit while also taking part in a shared, highly disciplined structure.

These monasteries soon had to be fortified for protection from raiding infiltrators from Libya, Bedouins the imperial Romans referred to as "barbarians." Such monastic fortresses had no gates: anyone who was to receive entry was pulled up over the wall in a basket. Saint Pachomius is widely considered the founder of Christian cenobitic monasticism, which emphasizes community life. He was succeeded by the famous Abba Antonius, or Saint Anthony the Abbot, whose temptations in the desert ignited the imagination of Western painters; and Paul of Thebes, the First Hermit, namesake of a large monastery on the Red Sea. The Coptic Church's constitution was composed in these monasteries. Those deemed ready to leave the "world" and its temptations behind were called upon to lead the church as bishops, and thus return to the "world" and minister to it. Ever since then the authority of the Coptic Church has rested primarily with monks and less with married diocesan priests, who can never become bishops.

It's no wonder, then, that believers seek out a connection with monks, and that pilgrimages to cloisters are among the highlights of their lives. The regular trips the Twenty-One made to monasteries to give confession and celebrate major festivals were common habits followed by many Copts, who hold the conviction that monasteries are the place to experience the church in its purest, most undisturbed state. The underlying reason is clear: behind monastery walls, the pressure exerted by the Islamic majority grows weaker. Here the world seems to consist solely of Copts; monasteries are essentially small Coptic states ruled by an abbot-bishop who functions much like a priestly king.

This has become all the more true since the notable expansion of Egypt's cloisters in the twentieth century. On the campus of the main monasteries in Wadi Natrun, one first has to wander among the many large new build-ings – churches, guesthouses, assembly halls, and the monastic blocks that replaced the old cells, which had no water or electricity – before finding the ancient structures dating back to the first millennium. Few tourists come here in search of historical works of art, as travel guides have given few stars to the local treasures. Even the desert has disappeared; the monks have turned it into verdant farm-land despite Saint Macarius of Egypt's prophesy, which warned that if the desert were touched the monasteries would die.

For the time being, at least, this does not seem to be the case. In fact, it looks as though the Western Benedictine approach has begun to permeate these monasteries, which have become centers of culture and development. In keeping with this, some grand new monasteries only accept postulants who have completed their military service and education; nowadays, many doctors and engineers have joined the monks' ranks.

The first time I set foot in a Coptic monastery was in 2002, under President Mubarak's administration, thir-teen years before my journey to visit the families of the Twenty-One. In Luxor, on the western bank of the Nile near Medinet Habu, the great temple of Ramses III, I looked from a rooftop terrace out over the desert, which began a few steps from the front door. In the distance rose a cliff housing the tombs of ancient queens and nobles; to their right stood the huge pillars of the great hypostyle hall in the largely preserved temple; behind them, a swath of palm trees waved. It was almost like being on the beach. From this densely populated area I gazed into the void.

But then I spotted something – it was difficult to make out what it was at first. It loomed far in the distance, and did not seem to consist of rocks or sand dunes, but looked instead like a manmade structure built with a material the same color as sand. These mounds piqued my curiosity enough so that, early one morning, I set out to have a closer look. It was rough going, hiking through the rocky desert. I felt as if I were stumbling in the direction of something that, for quite some time, remained a vague apparition, far away. There wasn't a single footprint or tire track in sight and the odd mounds, much farther than I had guessed from the rooftop, disappeared from view as I staggered onward.

Then I found myself standing before an adobe wall surmounted by thorns. I clambered onto a nearby boulder and peered over it into a garden of petite palms and dense hedges – a thick layer of green-black and gray-green foliage, orange trees, beds of beans and potatoes, crumbling garden sheds, and a well.

Nowhere does a garden radiate such promise as in the desert. The harsh sun was filtered into a thousand soft specks of light. In such a place one immediately grasps that life is synonymous with shade, humidity, coolness, and the scent of foliage. It was, as gardens go, unkempt and poorly designed, but at the same time it was paradise. Now, whenever I hear the word "garden," I think of that oasis. There wasn't a soul in sight, and the silence was so thick I was startled by a stone that came loose from the wall and pattered to the ground, making a noise so well-defined and overpowering, it sounded like we were in a recording studio.

I looked for an entrance but found the wall impenetrable, and its crown of thorns a formidable deterrent to scaling it. Farther along I came across an opening: a door left ajar. I entered and found myself in a clean-swept courtyard. At the far end stood a church, a long, low building with several little domes – the mounds I had seen from my rooftop terrace.

The interior revealed an unfamiliar floor plan, twice as wide as it was deep, with five aisles and rough-hewn, low pillars. The small domes rose from these pillars, culminating in small oculi. These round holes allowed sunbeams to pierce the twilight, like headlights at night or the rays one sees in an old *hamam*, where beams of light from the vaulted ceiling cut through the vapor of the baths. The *hurus* was a long wooden wall with crumbling inlays and five gates, each closed off by a red velvet curtain in a glittering plastic protector. As in a mosque, the floor was completely covered in worn carpets. The paintings, which hung askew, were prints of Italian Madonnas in the style of Carlo Dolci – as popular here as elsewhere – and portraits of the Blessed Virgin, such as Our Lady of Graces, first seen by Marian visionary Catherine Labouré on the Rue du Bac in Paris. Close to the *hurus* I saw a hunched-over old woman veiled in black, who briefly looked toward me and then quickly turned back.

After the brutal beating I had taken from the sun, standing under these domes was a relief. Outside I recognized the cells, monastic quarters domed just like the church, stretching along the walls like a line of dwarves. I was convinced this monastery hadn't changed much since the fourth century. The relatively new Western imagery didn't interfere with this impression – in fact, the prints only reinforced it.

Not far from the monastery stood the grandiose temple of Ramses III, with its massif-like pillars and impeccable stonemasonry. It was already ancient when this little monastery was founded, but by the time the church was built the locals – who, as Copts, were conscious of their connection to previous generations – had long since forgotten everything their forebears had known about architecture. It had marked a new beginning, but then stayed that way. The law of the land was longstanding immutability, and this law clearly obliged the monastery's inhabitants, of whom I saw only the old woman. Poverty, silence, and isolation would help them overcome any troubles they might encounter over the course of their short human lives. This was "Thebais" in both the literal and figurative sense. Here, the idea that history has an endpoint, and that one could nonetheless persevere even long after that point passed, struck me as entirely conceivable.

That was 2002. Now here I was back in Egypt again, this time following in the footsteps of the martyrs. After having visited both the oldest and at the same time most modern monasteries in Wadi Natrun, with its teeming pilgrims, bus depots, and giant construction sites for even bigger complexes amid the green desert – humming centers of modern Coptic culture with multiple concrete domes and church towers whose crosses are visible for miles – I remembered the little desert monastery I had visited thirteen years before. Hadn't I come close to the origins of the Coptic Church there? I described the monastery to my travel companions, who told me it was a convent, by no means unknown, and an important place. It houses the relics of one of Saint Joseph's cousins, who traveled after the Holy Family following Herod's death to tell them that the mortal danger they had fled had finally come to an end. Clearly, the flight into Egypt branched out and grew new roots here, with numerous side stories and secondary characters. The monastery's name (in Arabic) is El Mohareb. It is dedicated to Saint Tawadros, Theodore in Greek, the original dragon slayer; Saint George, a Roman soldier and martyr, has been celebrated as such only since the Middle Ages.

I had gone in search of timelessness, but was discovering just how long thirteen years can really feel – like an eternity. Standing on the same terrace from which I had discovered the cloister during my first trip, I again spotted El Mohareb on the border between cultivated fields and desert. This time I noticed policemen in black uniforms guarding the Temple of Medinet Habu, rifles with wooden stocks tucked under their arms. Toward the mountain range bordering the desert, I saw jeeps driving up and down the road on patrol. A policeman later told me that Islamist guerrillas lurked in the mountains. Was that why the entire range was lined with spotlights that gave the landscape an oddly operatic feel by night?

The monastery was now much easier to recognize from the terrace: a large sheet-metal awning stood in front of it, shielding a police car and two guards on folding chairs from the sun. A high concrete wall divided the monastery grounds from the stony, treeless land that surrounded them, but then subsided in the sand beyond. As night fell, the cloister's cupolas looked like a bunch of turtle shells under the bright floodlights. The surroundings were still barren, but the monastery itself looked less lonely. Who could reproach the nuns for requesting protection? And wasn't it consoling to know they had been granted it?

The road to El Mohareb no longer led through open land, but now ran along the bleak wall. Upon arrival, I counted some fifty cars parked under the canopy. A guesthouse had been built in the courtyard, and in front of it was a covered, open-air hall with lined-up tables and benches. A mountain of shoes lay by the church door – just like in mosques, people take off their shoes before entering Coptic churches, at least during communion. A Copt would rephrase that: "In mosques, people take off their shoes just like they do in our churches, since our traditions are several centuries older." Mass was in progress, and many people sat on the floor and leaned against pillars. Here in the countryside, older men wore *jellabiyas* and turbans. The latter do not have to be removed in holy places, as they are not viewed the same way hats and caps are in the West.

I hardly recognized the room this time. The church had been lavishly restored. The plaster and thick layers of oil paint had been stripped away, and the masonry was now exposed. Many of the stones clearly came from the temple in Medinet Habu: hieroglyphs, ibises, and a beautiful wing from Maat, goddess of truth and justice, had all entered the new sanctuary as spolia. The temple had long been a quarry for peasants, and how much of it has survived centuries of ransacking says a lot about its sheer size. The Carlo Dolci Madonna had disappeared, and newly painted archaic icons shone on the partition, but there were still some old eighteenth-century icons. They had apparently been relegated to a shed and then restored, because their surface was now glossy as lacquer.

On my first visit I had seen only one nun, but now a large group of women between the ages of thirty and sixty, with healthy peasant faces, sat to the right of the main hall, in black robes and headscarves. They were the oldest people in the room. The large crowd of believers consisted primarily of children and adolescents, some accompanied by a father or mother. They would all eat together in the open-air hall after Mass – a fast-day meal of bean soup, as had been done for millennia – and later, religious lessons would be held. The nuns cooked for everyone, and sold honey, candles, and portraits of the church patriarchs in the monastery shop.

El Mohareb was abuzz with activity, but something was missing: Where were the dense blacks and greens of the garden, that chiaroscuro kingdom that had so enchanted me? I had especially looked forward to seeing it again, hoping to spend some time in its peace. But the garden was no more. The nuns had had to give it up, along with the small wheat field that provided the grain from which they baked bread for the Eucharist. The government had recently banned farming in the desert, perhaps for good reason, but it meant that only a few dried-up stalks remained of the garden which, for me, had so unforgettably embodied the sheer fertility of the cloister's isolation.

Elsewhere these kinds of changes, brought on by the blossoming of newly active communities, had taken place decades ago – El Mohareb had just slumbered a little longer. This delay allowed me to see the development of the Coptic Church over the last century compressed into a solid decade, right before my own eyes. The decay of previous centuries was nowhere in sight. This was no longer "Thebais." Anyone who, like me, had witnessed its previous state – anyone who had felt its enchantment, its connection to an existence beyond the grave, and seen it not simply as a form of fossilization or standstill, but rather recognized a sacred principle within it – had to view this change with ambivalence.

Were these signs of a rebirth, or the beginning of something entirely new and different? If a body that has shown no signs of life suddenly begins to stir after a seemingly eternal immobility, and then begins to run faster and faster, it can be jarring – and that is exactly how Muslim observers view this development. But many Copts, too, wonder where the journey is headed. How much of what has been preserved by that long slumber will they be able to take with them into the future?

Hany

17

Wonders Old and New

ONE OF EL-AOUR's neighboring villages, Al Bayahu, looks a little bigger and more prosperous. In the heart of the village is a church that, at first glance, doesn't look much different from the one in El-Aour, but has particular signif-icance. Its patron saint is an abbot, Iskhirun, who lived during the earliest years of Coptic Christianity in Lower Egypt, in the Nile Delta. And that is where this church was built, long ago.

During one of the early waves of persecution – under the Persians, or perhaps the Arabs – seven couples, engaged to be wed, had taken refuge in the church and barricaded the door. Their persecutors set the structure on fire, where-upon the seven couples prepared for the horrific death that awaited them by praying. Miraculously, they were spared the worst, their ardent faith in God's presence wonderfully rewarded. Just as the smoke threatened to overtake them, angels swooped in, lifted the church from its foundations and, right before the eyes of their perplexed persecutors, carried it through the skies to Upper Egypt, where things were calmer, and set it down in Al Bayahu. The rescued couples then strode out into their newfound freedom and started new lives in their new home.

Amazed, I looked around – this church was supposedly moved here more than a thousand years ago? The space

I saw had to have been from the 1970s, at most. The only ancient-looking object in the entire place was a reliquary off the side aisle containing the bones of Saint Iskhirun framed by two short, unfinished pillars supporting a dome carved from a single large block. The dignified priest, who had a thin white beard, noticed my astonishment and calmly confirmed that, indeed, the miraculously transposed church had been demolished because it was dilapidated and too small. He considered the spaciousness of this shabby, poorly decorated, newer structure with an expression of contentment. After all, the reliquary had been preserved, and outside in the courtyard there were still a few ornamental stones the congregation had decided to save. A famous spring had also appeared there, which had sprung up on the same day of the miraculous angelic *translatio*. He handed me a plastic bottle of water, saying it would bestow blessings and health.

Didn't the transfer of an entire church, intact, across hundreds of miles, constitute such a tremendous instance of supernatural intervention here on earth that the building simply had to be preserved? No one here saw it like that. There was no concern for conservation, even out of curiosity; no desire to have the ancient stones archaeologically examined. The idea of preserving such objects as ancient bearers of witness to their faith was alien not only to this priest, but to everyone here. Back in Samalut I had expressed a desire to visit an old church, for once, and that is when I was told about Al Bayahu. In the eyes of the people awaiting me in front of the building, the fact that something new had taken the place of the ancient church did not at all detract from its holy essence.

I did not manage to mask my disappointment. The aged pastor had a young, newly ordained priest at his side, standing tall in his wide black cassock. He had been born and raised in Al Bayahu, and had returned right after graduation.

"Could you spend your whole life here?"

His question caught me mid-thought, just as I was secretly trying to imagine what it would be like to never be able to leave this place. What would it be like to move into one of the tall, new, yet already decrepit houses with cows and goats living on the ground floor?

My polite white lie – "Sure, why not?" – must have been utterly transparent.

His smile betrayed a touch of mockery. "I actually will live here until the end of my days!" Convinced he would be able to persevere in this village, amid the thickly swarming flies, even though he had gotten to know and maybe even appreciate Cairo during his studies, he seemed to feel superior.

It would be all too easy to assume the ever-sharper contrast between metropolis and farmland follows the European pattern: pious peasants here, liberal agnostic city dwellers there. But the great miracles that have accompanied the Coptic Church's difficult path through history, and continue to do so today, do not exclude contemporary Cairo.

For many Copts, a miracle is always the most obvious explanation for any favorable event. New visions are constantly reported, one after the other – it's as if the Mother of God and all the saints were perpetually pushing into the earthly realm to reach their Coptic children. Saint Pachomius, a great mystic, tried very early on to relegate such apparitions to their right place; speaking to a some-what fanatical monk, he tried to help him understand what really matters: "The most wonderful vision is when you look into the face of your fellow human being and see the purity and deep humility of his heart reflected back at you.

Can there be any more beautiful vision than to see invisible God living in man as his temple?"

Purity and humility, however, can be rare even in Egypt – certainly rarer, in any case, than the presence of the Blessed Mother, who strengthens monks and nuns throughout the nation in prayer, heals the sick, and facilitates the construction of new churches. Cairo has had two major Marian apparitions over the past century, witnessed by thousands of Christians and Muslims. One was even photographed, and you can see her dark figure in a long veil, with tilted head, standing like a blurry silhouette on the church roof. Both appearances occurred in the midst of dangerous political crises: the first came just after Egypt lost the Six-Day War against Israel; the second came during the ongoing struggle between Pope Shenouda III and President Sadat regarding the Copts' civil rights; the pope was banished to Wadi Natrun and was unable to return to Cairo for many years.

Given the excitement these silent apparitions sparked in Egyptians, the question of what "caused" them is too simplistic for most Copts. From their point of view, the ups and downs of history are merely temporary conditions: no victory or defeat of life's good cause is permanent. Right up until the last judgment, the entire earth will remain a battlefield, but it only mirrors the simultaneous, invisible battle being waged between angels and demons. Again and again, it is angels who help believers overcome evil. Even then, however, victory is only temporary. If humankind prevails against the forces of darkness, it does so with the help of the angels – but if humankind is beaten and destroyed, that, too, does not happen without them. The sole purpose of salvation from earth's dangers is this: having been led to one's mortal downfall, one may now attain the heavenly palm frond of victory in the afterlife. Doom and salvation are equivalent, and both are evidence that our prayers are heard. Temporary, earthly salvation serves only to strengthen humankind for the final defeat. Indeed, it ideally sharpens one's senses, especially in defeat, making one better able to recognize the presence of the divine.

This is the spirit out of which tales regarding the Twenty-One's imprisonment arise. One recurring story involves an unknown witness, a guard who, impressed by his captives' faithful steadfastness, is said to have converted to Christianity. It is reminiscent of many ancient tales – the first concerning the Roman centurion who stood under the cross and confessed, right after Jesus' death, "Truly, this was the Son of God." He is followed by many others through history who, confronted with the sight of a martyr, switched sides and turned from persecutor to persecuted.

Every day of their weeks-long imprisonment, the Twenty-One were tortured and beaten, and every morning they awoke healed and unscarred. It didn't sound to me like a report from 2015, but more like a tale from Jacobus de Varagine's *Golden Legend*, in which the suffering of the martyrs is interwoven with countless miraculous details, much as nuns' monastic work once entailed winding martyrs' bones up in gold wire and flowers. And this mysterious witness leads us back still further, as early as Acts, when he says that the Twenty-One prayed incessantly and sang liturgical hymns during their imprisonment: "And when they sang the *Kyrie eleison*, the mountains quaked." Similarly, in Acts, Luke writes of the assembled apostles' prayer, which he quotes as follows: "'Now, Lord, consider their threats and enable your servants to speak your word with great boldness.' . . . After they prayed, the place where they were meeting was shaken."

Even those who are not fundamentally opposed to the possibility of miracles will be most likely to accept them, the further in the past they occurred. Our historical consciousness is strongly influenced by ruptures and breaks in tradition that cast the eras of European history in sharp contrast. This has weakened our sense of historical continuity – our sense that the past contains the story of our origins and that, consciously or unconsciously, it continues in and with us. For the priests who told me about the miracles surrounding the Twenty-One, on the other hand, it was precisely this continuity that was decisive: from their point of view, the dramatic breaks between each era, so real to Western students of history, simply never took place. In their eyes, nothing separates our present day from that of the Diocletian persecutions – the times are in no way different. They are as convinced today as they were in the first centuries that when it comes to a Christian's life, the same law of succession applies: each must bear Jesus' cross. And therefore they take it for granted that God surrounded their newest martyrs with the same signs of grace he bestowed upon the oldest. Miracles did not save the Twenty-One from decapitation, but they did prove that their sacrifice had made them Christlike and was therefore accepted.

And because, from their perspective, there is no such thing as a past in the sense of anything or anyone being dead, gone, and utterly untethered from their faith – from Jesus' ascension onward, the world has lived in a perpetual present – preserving the old church the angels had carried to Upper Egypt wasn't considered important. Further, a rigorous archaeological investigation would only have distracted from the fact that something similar could happen again at any moment. Christians will perpetually be tested, right up until the second coming of Jesus. But their trials are only superficial, vacillating between lighter and darker times – in truth, there is only one great Advent, the Last Judgment the world is still awaiting.

As I stood and looked at the new church, embarrassed that I could not admire it as expected, the words of a monk

I had met on Mount Athos came to mind: "Don't forget, it was the shepherds who saw the angels at Jesus' birth – the magi only saw the star." The magi were the intellectuals, and seeing the stars offered them some knowledge of God, but those who saw the angels were granted a very different degree of certainty.

Malak (the elder)

18

With the Zabbaleens of Mokattam Village

UNTIL RECENTLY CAIRO HAD no municipal waste collection, and yet the trash was disposed of – for the most part, at least. There was just enough left that you would never accuse the city of being overly hygienic. Donkeys laden with garbage bags trotted through the streets, and the odors trailing behind them betrayed the contents. The smell of trash is different from the venerable stench of latrines and tanneries – it's a smell that doesn't naturally exist, reeking of smeary plastics, of deathly dust and sterility.

Although municipal garbage trucks now make the rounds, the rickety old donkey-drawn carts haven't entirely disappeared. Little boys steer them through dense traffic, taking visible joy in weaving between buses and trucks, and dodging the black plumes of diesel exhaust. Some even go on foot, carrying bags bigger than their own bodies, crammed with empty bottles and crumpled-up snack bags. Their destination is a neighborhood bordering the desert sands, near the old citadel, at the foot of the mountains. Muslims refer to this range as the Mokattam, or "broken mountain," because, as legend would have it, this massif looming over the city was not always located on this spot.

As their simple language suggests, Coptic Christians
love to interpret holy scriptures quite literally. What justifies theologians in categorizing Jesus' every provocation as
unlikely, symbolic, or allegorical, anyway? "Truly I tell you,
if you have faith as small as a mustard seed, you can say to
this mountain, 'Move from here to there,' and it will move.
Nothing will be impossible for you." In the year 975 these
words of Christ, as recorded in the Gospel of Matthew,
triggered a dispute between the vizier of the Fatimid
caliphate and Ebn-Zaraa, Pope Abraham of Alexandria.
The caliph settled the theological debate on his own: either
the pope would successfully prove the truth of this promise
or he would be beheaded. The pope requested three days
to fast and pray, and was granted them. As he prayed, the
Blessed Virgin appeared to him in Saint Mary's Church
El-Mu'allaqah, the "Hanging Church," above the Babylon
Fortress of Old Cairo, and ordered him to seek out a
one-eyed man. The one-eyed man was found, and became
known as Simon the Tanner. Simon, too, had chosen to take
the Gospels literally and – in obedience to another of Jesus'
statements, also recorded by Matthew – had gouged out his
eye because it had "caused him to stumble." No one had a
greater right to remind God of his promise than someone
who had inflicted such harm to his own body out of reliance on scripture. Upon Simon's prayers, and after the pope
had given his blessing, the Mokattam Mountain rose three
times and moved three kilometers, finally landing in its
present location. On the way, it broke into three parts.

The fractures that attest to its migration are easily recognizable. Early on, in a grotto high as a cathedral, a small
Marian shrine was built to commemorate the mountain's
miraculous relocation. But it was only in the twentieth
century that the mountain, grotto, and sandy region that
spread out before it became a center of Coptic life – and at
the same time a symbol of the misery and splendor of the

Coptic faith in its astonishing perseverance on the dark side of history.

When people talk about Copts, they seldom neglect to mention their wealth. Yes, there are some very wealthy Coptic families. And in proportion to their small number, their share of the national wealth may be astonishing or revolting, depending on how one feels about them. Copts earned handsomely under the British Protectorate, in particular, because the colonial rulers preferred to rely on fellow Christians. But most Copts are not rich, and many are poor. The five thousand peasant Copts from Upper Egypt and the Faiyum Oasis who moved to Cairo together in 1960 – several large extended families in search of a live-lihood – were not just poor, they were destitute. But they had not lost their resourcefulness. No one had been waiting for them in Cairo; they had to look out for themselves and learn how to get by in the jungle of the already wildly growing metropolis. They raised swine, the very embodi-ment of impurity according to Muslim and Jewish dietary laws, proving that the traditional ban on pork is not, as is commonly thought today, due solely to the hot Middle Eastern climate. It might not have been easy for unwelcome people to find food in Cairo, but it was easy to raise pigs on the city's garbage.

Thus the rural emigrants became *zabbaleen* – literally "garbage people" and, by extension, "garbage collectors" – and filled an urgent need in the urban community. As in ancient times, men and boys scavenged for and collected the garbage, and women and girls sorted it. Then the famous singer Umm Kulthum, annoyed by the piles of garbage accumulating around her villa – who could blame her? – asked President Nasser, one of her many devotees, to expel the *zabbaleen*. It was on his orders that they moved to the outskirts of the city, where the miraculous broken mountain now rests. There was no running water or sewage system there, but that didn't intimidate the frugal newcomers. The land surrounding the rocky outcrop was incredibly inhospitable, yet at the same time the blessed mountain made it holy terrain.

There are now eighty thousand people living there. Their houses have six floors. At ground level, the open floor plan facilitates the careful sorting of the collected garbage, which is tied up into big bales. The stench is breathtaking, though luckily, smells are one of the few unpleasant things one quickly gets used to. And smack in the middle of these garbage heaps lie the butcheries, complete with skinned sheep on open-air display. The fact that Saint Simon, a man employed in the foul-smelling tannery trade, became the patron and protector of this settlement seems fitting enough.

Following a 2009 swine flu outbreak, the city culled all extant herds and prohibited citizens from raising pigs – though as with most administrative measures in Egypt, enforcement was haphazard, and the results predictable. In other words, there are still plenty of pigs, now kept mainly in basements or on rooftop terraces. Still, because of the narrow streets and tall buildings the air is so thick that it made me not only want to flee, but also change my clothes as soon as possible. There is no way to gloss over it: Mokattam is a hideous place, and the awe that its gloomy, underworldly aspects inspire is of an infernal sort.

On that note, one cannot forget that this neighborhood, a city unto itself, has long been a symbol of the boldness and valor bestowed on its people by their considerable degree of success. I didn't fully understood this until I followed a narrow road full of potholes and putrid puddles to where it led through a gate onto the rocky plateau spreading out under the jagged rock wall towering above.

Here a surprise awaited me: my surroundings had suddenly changed from hell to heaven. Beyond the narrow access road, a vast expanse opened up onto an endlessly broad panorama. Below me the tall houses of the so-called garbage village leaned toward one another, each crowned by precarious-looking scaffolding supporting a little hut – the pigeon loft.

Pigeon keeping is a common hobby among Egyptian peasants, and these rural people brought the practice into the city with them. Just as in ancient Greece, where doves and pigeons were considered the birds of Aphrodite, here, too, they are highly sought after as an aphrodisiac. (At rural weddings neighbors traditionally bring fifty roast pigeons stuffed with rice, with which the bride and groom are then locked up for three days!) Above the pigeon lofts, huge flocks fly in circles against the rosy sky until their respective keeper whistles a unique tune to summon them home.

Turning away from these bizarre bird-filled towers, I spotted the Monastery of Saint Simon the Tanner. One in a series of cave churches in the rock wall, its entrance looks like a gaping mouth of stone leading into the depths. Here, over the last few years, half in the open air and half in the mass of rock, a church that holds several thousand people has been built. As in ancient Greek theaters, the seats take the shape of a large shell, and where the skene would have been stands an iconostasis closing off the rest of the cave. The altar is hidden deeper inside the mountain, behind a red velvet curtain. It is a place of miracles and apparitions: one small cave contains the wheelchairs of the many paralytics who have been healed here, and above the iconostasis a bas-relief of the Virgin with the infant Jesus, made by no human hand, has been discovered; it has since been reworked by a Polish sculptor. Here, again, I couldn't help but notice how little the Copts care about documenting or preserving original, authentic phenomena. In a world made

entirely of miracles, you don't have to depend on any one
manifestation for very long: you can be confident that the
next one is soon to come.

The cave churches of Mokattam are the site of weekday
prayers held to support the exorcism of the possessed and
mentally ill. The task of expelling evil spirits – one of the
first Jesus gave to his church, and one that is mostly treated
as a source of embarrassment in the Western world – is
understood here, as in the Gospels, as one of a priest's
primary duties. Several priests in black cassocks perform
this service in the cave churches, which now have their
own bishop; in fact, the garbage village has since been
elevated to a diocese. After all, it has grown from a wild
settlement of wretched huts into a thriving district so well
organized that it sells its sorted garbage to China. A second,
completely closed-off cave has become a meeting hall that
can seat hundreds of people; instructing the laity is another
important mission of the modern Coptic Church, and yet
another point of a difference with the Western church,
which seems to have given up the task of religious education as readily as it has the expulsion of evil spirits.

To me, the history of the *zabbaleen* in the holy cave
seems a good example of the Coptic Church's resurgence
in the twentieth century. Are not the garbage-collecting
boys, their skin so thoroughly steeped in dirt that no
brush could ever clean it, a symbol of the hopeless position the Copts have often found themselves in after 1,400
years of oppression, and the exhaustion of their very last
resources – but also of their resilience? Without that, how
would it ever have been possible for them to regroup,
summon what little strength remained, and mobilize their
once-formidable forces?

An outsider's eye might allow him to discover many
things hidden from (or simply invisible to) an insider, but
it certainly doesn't help him assess the amount of energy

that lies dormant at the core of such a movement. Even less so if, compelled by earthly logic, he feels obliged to exclude supernatural sources of strength as an explanation. Arching high above the vast neighborhood of trash, hasn't this enormous old cave and its supposedly miraculous powers already brought the *zabbaleen* success? Once a neglected space, it now hosts plentiful flocks of pilgrims – a transformation that directly results from the massive increase in the Coptic population at the foot of the cliffs. The image of the Virgin lay dormant in the rock for more than a millennium before it was discovered, and over that millennium, the Copts became fewer and fewer, poorer and poorer, ever weaker and more despised. Without any rights or privileges, they endured and eked out an existence on the margins of Muslim society. They were an uneducated, obscure lot. And no Copt who has studied the historical facts cares to recall just how far back that condition stretches in time. Of course, a community's view of political history and science as irrelevant also has its advantages. . . .

The power exerted by the Blessed Virgin and Mother of God in Mokattam also has a highly protective function. One can view the rocky terrain above the city not only as a sanctuary, but also as a fortress. Few fighters could ever make it through the narrow entrance of its stone gate. Every now and then along the way there, the young men leading me pointed out how well the place could be defended from attack. True, the Pope of Alexandria and his bishops regularly urge their flocks not to reciprocate violence with violence. But the words of Mokattam's young Copts suggest that they are determined not to accept any more persecution without putting up a good fight.

Malak (the younger)

19

A Coptic Fantasia

WHAT MIGHT THINGS LOOK LIKE if Christian Egypt
had never been conquered by the Arabs? A question like
this is posed in vain, considering the sheer weight of historical fact. It is impossible to imagine the world without
Islam, which, within a relatively short period, took North
Africa, Asia Minor, Persia, Northern India, and present-day
Indonesia by storm – a vexing tempest that both seemed to
have come out of nowhere and also seemed like it had always
been there. Looking at the Western church and its cultural
triumphs, however, and noting how favorable conditions
were for the early Coptic Church, the latent possibilities of
the latter become clearer – an unrealized potential that was
perpetually stifled by the political situation.

Culturally, Alexandria was Rome's equal: it was the
center of Hellenistic Judaism and a capital of philosophy,
literature, and religion. Gnostic speculation and syncretic
rites, mysterious cults and Platonic schools, as well as
the traditional ancient Egyptian religion's great hope in
the hereafter – all helped pave the way for Christianity.
The Coptic Church was founded by Saint Mark the
Evangelist, who is considered a pupil of Peter; it claims
to be as "Petrine" as Rome, and its patriarchate is one of
the four – later five – patriarchates of the early church. The
Patriarch of Alexandria has held the official title of pope

since 249, which is nearly one hundred years longer than the Bishop of Rome.

Diocletian-era attempts to quite literally eradicate this new church proved just how quickly, thoroughly, and deeply it had become rooted in Egypt's soil – the old emperor himself had to admit failure. But, following in the wake of the empire's division into east and west by the sons of Theodosius the Great, an establishmentarian impulse within the broader church posed an even greater threat to Coptic freedom. The Patriarch of Constantinople's attempt to subjugate the Copts, depose their patriarch, and excommunicate the Coptic Church as a whole at the Council of Chalcedon forced the Coptic patriarch underground. Ever since, the Great Schism has divided Alexandria from Constantinople and Rome.

But still, try to imagine the impossible: the Islamic conquest did not take place, and after a while Byzantium grew too weak to maintain its hold against Egyptians' resistance, just as the later Ottomans were too weak to assure dominion over Egypt. Then a new day dawned in which the independent Coptic Church became the equal of both Rome and Byzantium, with its own solid foundation laid by important theologians, its own great monasteries, and its own history of suffering from which it only emerged stronger. All this, sprung from the rich humus of ancient Egyptian culture, with its unique architecture and art and its successful fusion with Greek culture. After all, one of the most beautiful temples in Egypt, originally part of a complex on the Island of Philae in the Nile near Aswan, was first built under Emperor Trajan.

Wouldn't such conditions have been more than favorable for the development of a high Coptic culture? After its liberation by Emperor Constantine, the young Coptic Church initially acted aggressively against pagan cults. The horrific low point of this wave of fanaticism was the murder of the renowned Neoplatonist philosopher Hypatia, who was viciously killed by a mob of angry monks. The Serapeum of Alexandria, a temple dedicated to the syncretic Greco-Egyptian deity Serapis, where Hypatia had taught, was destroyed. But from its ruins people found and saved stones with hieroglyphs of the ankh – a cross topped by a circle instead of a straight vertical line – the symbol for life. The Copts adapted this sign to create their very own Coptic cross, and convinced themselves that the conquered Greco-Egyptian religion was as connected to Christianity as a germ is to wheat. Even in Greece and the rest of the West the rediscovery of ancient philosophy and art has almost always been preceded by a phase in which ancient documents and other attestations of the earlier culture were destroyed.

And yet, had the Copts been left undisturbed, their renaissance might have come faster and more easily – after all, they were not so far removed from the preeminent Greek philosophers. The Hellenistic mummy portraits created chiefly for Copts and excavated in the Faiyum Oasis show that Egypt had its own mature, highly colorful, painterly realism – an art the Copts could have further developed, especially since, after separating from Byzantium, they were spared the iconoclasm that swept through other traditions and thus developed no such church-controlled, theologically integrated iconic tradition.

A Coptic Bramante, a Coptic Brunelleschi who could have produced a new architecture from Greco-Egyptian hybrid forms – is this really so unthinkable? The Coptic pope, in his palace at Alexandria, surrounded by statues of Ptah, Isis, falcon-headed Horus, and lion-headed Sekhmet, just as the Roman pope keeps statues of Apollo, Mercury, and Jupiter in the Vatican Palace – is that really such a grotesque vision? An anti-liturgical heresy, a Coptic Luther, a Coptic Reformation – are those entirely out of the question? And all the other stages of Western ecclesiastical history – enlightenment and secularization, first fought over, then accepted – would those have been impossibilities for the Copts? These may sound merely like seductive thought experiments inspired by rich material, but they are also proof of our inclination to confuse the culture produced by Christianity with Christianity itself. The Christian faith has demonstrated an immeasurable cultural fruitfulness that, considering the circumstances of its creation in the Holy Land, is a marvel impossible to overstate. But at its core it remains quite independent of this culture.

The Western world has long given the church a leading role, and the church has filled this role through both good and bad times; it has taken part in the ups and downs of European history, unleashed vast creative forces, and for a long time even saw itself as a hero. The Coptic Church, in its seemingly hopeless struggle for survival, looks wretched in comparison. But now, in the wake of the Constantinian era, in which the Copts only participated for the first three centuries, the Western church must ask itself whether it is as well prepared to spread the faith in an increasingly secularized world as the Coptic Church is. The Copts have clearly had a head start: they have long had to withstand oppression by a hostile majority, and have an intimate collective knowledge of martyrdom. Due to this history, they have endured countless setbacks for more than a millennium; "development," the buzzword of Western civilization, has been denied them. And yet they have not disappeared and have not grown numb; on the contrary, they have kept the apostolic heritage of early Christianity alive. Not only that but, since the initial Persian and later Islamic conquest, they have also resisted the temptation to wield power in the name of God.

Christianity is not a myth. It relies on historical events that actually took place, and therefore must constantly look back to its beginnings. Nowhere can this be done, without depending too much on archeology, as easily as with the Copts; for early Christianity is alive and well in their midst, whereas in other churches it must be laboriously excavated, with often dubious outcomes.

The Copts have relevant experience when it comes to the future of Christianity, too. How might Christianity look, and continue on, once societal majorities and governments are no longer tolerant and benevolent, but hostile? And what if Christians are denied the ability to participate in public life simply because they refuse to submit or convert to another religion? Could it perhaps be that the path the Western church has taken over the centuries has just been a huge, highly eventful detour that is now leading right back to the fork in the road where the Coptic Church has patiently persevered this entire time?

Tawadros

20

New Cairo – A Mirage

ONE DAY MOHAMMED, the defense lawyer, introduced me to his friend and client, a painter of a certain age. She looked vaguely Italian and had spent much of her life in London and Paris. Her return to Cairo hadn't been entirely voluntary. She had actually wanted to leave Egypt, the land of her ancestors, behind. She was astonished to find that wearing the veil, a badge of the lower class in her childhood, was beginning to find acceptance in the middle and upper classes. She was from a family of intellectuals, and her mother had never covered her hair. But when Western collectors' interest in her large, somewhat abstractly speckled paintings had begun to diminish, and at the same time rampant inflation was eating away at her parents' savings, she moved back. She still had an apartment in Zamalek, on Gezira Island in the Nile, which her mother had lived in previously. Leases can be inherited in Egypt, so Cairenes lucky enough to have an old lease can live there for next to nothing.

The neighborhood's magnificent belle époque and art deco apartments are worth seeing. In the elevator in the painter's apartment building, I caught a glimpse into the deep shaft through a few holes in the floor. The stairwell light was broken, which partially hid further neglect and decay. But her apartment itself – decorated with baroque

Egyptian furniture and bric-a-brac accumulated over decades, and lit by old chandeliers with only a few of the original crystals intact – was so cozy that I was sorry we had to leave again so soon.

The painter was eager to show me something, "something gorgeous." Even talking about the treat I was in for made her heart beat faster, she said. She was referring to Cairo not as it currently stood – "Yeah, yeah, I'm sure you've seen everything in the guidebooks" – but rather the Cairo to come. The previous day she had bought a sweater in this future Cairo, but she had felt indecisive and ultimately dissatisfied by her purchase. So she was going back to exchange it, and if I went along, she was sure I would not regret the experience. London was over for her – that was the past – but one of the things she had loved about London was now available right down the road in Cairo, and it had helped her get over the grief surrounding her unhappy move.

A small car was waiting for us outside. The painter introduced the silent, round man sitting at the wheel as her friend and assistant. We set off. Soon the city lights lay behind us, and we were engulfed in the blackness of a desert night.

Our destination – El-Qāhera el-Gedīda, or New Cairo – was less than an hour away on a busy highway. This new neighborhood was the government's attempt at relieving traffic in the older city center, whose seventeen million inhabitants keep it in a state of perpetual congestion. The plan was in keeping with local urban tradition: instead of laying out new developments in and around the old neighborhoods, they simply start a brand new town nearby; and when that one grows older and denser, the process continues. This is why Islamic Cairo developed next to the older districts of Jewish Cairo and Christian Cairo. Islamic Cairo borders Downtown Cairo, city of the Khedives, which was designed in the late nineteenth century by some of Europe's boldest architects. The opposite bank of the Nile is piled high with hotel and office skyscrapers. New Cairo, however, was built in the middle of the desert – an area that was, until recently, inhabited primarily by jackals.

The parking lots alone were as big as a city, and the interminable floodlit expanse was chock full of new midsize Korean cars. The immediate vicinity was dotted with brightly lit electronic billboards – circus-like, colorful islands of light – and beyond them spread a dark, deserted void. The bunker-like, big-box department stores looked large as airports, and above them shone the logos of IKEA, H&M, Zara, and Samsung. This shopping center had everything an urbane consumer from Shanghai or Jakarta, São Paulo or Moscow might desire.

Such a place is still a foreign entity in Egypt, but not completely unfamiliar. After all, the new martyrs of Upper Egypt were not the only ones who had gone abroad in search of work. Anyone who has the chance and the credentials – be it as a technician, doctor, IT specialist, or pharmacist – hopes to reach Saudi Arabia or the Gulf States, where they can enjoy a degree of prosperity that outshines even the most well-to-do European countries. The shopping malls now popping up in Egypt display a different, new type of material wealth that has nothing to do with the country's crowded old bazaars. Their products come from far and wide, and match the same tastes that are taking over the entire world. Despite their historic knowledge of human nature, shrewdness, and trade experience, the old Mediterranean merchant nations are enraptured by the goods on offer from the Swedes, for instance, who were also once a sleepy nation of aspiring peasants, though they apparently grasped the laws of this new economy faster and better than anyone else. As we wandered through the concrete forests of the underground parking garage in

search of an exit, I thought wistfully of the pillared forest of
the Al-Hussein Mosque near Al-Azhar University: sometimes perfect beauty and unholy ugliness are such close
neighbors.

Those who, like me, had been brought here unprepared
from Cairo's city center essentially experienced a form of
time travel. A moment ago we had been in the gloomy,
decadent, hulking old city driving along dilapidated belle
époque boulevards, past broken windows, dirty staircases,
and the dizzying alleyways of the Khan el-Kalili souk, where
both people and animals balance huge burdens as they
crowd between dingy teahouses filled with men smoking
water pipes and daydreaming. This is the old city of noble
mosques and magical necropolises to which peasants
flock from the countryside; the city of garbage-collecting
kids; the city of churches of all Christian denominations.
Seen from New Cairo, it was all one diminutive anthill
whose artful architecture could be crushed by the tire of
a shiny new car. From here the old city's constant hustle
and bustle – howling car horns, sermons streaming from
minaret loudspeakers, air so thick with dust and soot it
almost suffocates you – no longer seemed overwhelming,
but rather tender, almost fragile. It also felt defunct, like
a relic of history ready to be razed, a local product past its
expiration date, out of place in a new globalized market.

How long would it take for New Cairo to extinguish
the dirty flame keeping Old Cairo alive? How much time
would IKEA grant the thousands of furniture carvers
who were still busy gilding their wildly baroque chairs,
Churrigueresque versions of pharaonic luxury, in the old
bazaars? How long would the army of Cairene tailors still
sew their peculiarly square suits with wide, ruffled trou-
sers for local businessmen? In the long run, can a country
without oil or any other competitive industry attain the

glittering ideal embodied by the artificial cities of the Persian Gulf? Egypt still struggles to feed its ever-growing population; will its dream of joining the global ranks of consumers gobbling up and tossing out disposable goods lead to social catastrophe?

Earlier that morning, at a downtown teahouse, a man at the table next to mine, who introduced himself as an Islamic scholar, had given me a little lecture. He was a dignified gentleman with a thick white mustache, and smoked his hookah so conscientiously he could have been called a professional idler. "I know that people elsewhere say Egyptians are lazy, but that's not true. There are ethical reasons for our aversion to excessive enthusiasm. First and foremost, we find it rude to exert too much effort – doesn't it mean casting others aside? To pretend you're better than others and deserve more recognition – isn't that just ruthless?" I couldn't help wondering whether he had ever been to New Cairo. Or was he shielded from such disturbing visions by the gift of somnolence, like the Seven Sleepers of Ephesus, who retreated to a cave to escape religious persecution and only woke up again an entire century later?

But as I ran after the painter through glittering new designer handbag and shoe stores, something else stirred within me. I thought of the martyrs of El-Aour and their village, which didn't seem to exist in the same country as New Cairo. My stay with their families was still too close; I had gotten off the bus in Cairo after a ten-hour nighttime drive just the day before. Being plopped down so suddenly into a city seemingly built for nothing but shopping hit me like a blow to the head. I succumbed to a state of embarrassing confusion. The painter left me to my reveries. Having returned the sweater she had bought the day before, she was once more gripped by the intoxicating freedom of choice spread out before her. What an abundance of colors and styles from which to choose a new sweater! Or maybe she should get a silk blouse instead?

Letting my vivid imagination lead me, I tried to reconcile these two separate worlds – the Upper Egyptian village and the department store. How would the village's shabbily dressed peasant children have made their way through this shopping mall? Would they be amazed? Uncertain? Would they act as soberly as they did at the village market, and buy only what was useful and affordable? Or would this mall awaken latent desires buried deep within? Would they long for a share of this unfathomable abundance? More importantly, what else might this new yearning trigger within them? Would they continue to hold on to the things that had shaped their lives up to now, or would it all suddenly become alien to them amid this splendor?

Odd questions, I know! But my mind simply couldn't see how New Cairo and martyrdom fit together on the same planet, in the same country, at the same point in time. This wasn't a "yes or no," "this or that" world – I had entered the realm of "both, and. . . ." There were no final decisions here, just the endless right to exchange whatever you had just bought. This was the land of brightly lit nights and coolly air-conditioned days, right in the middle of the scorching desert. Here the enchanting cities of brass, princely palaces, and magic castles of old fairy tales all shriveled up – their closest material equivalents were the children's toys on display. The mall's crystal palace-inspired atria and stainless-steel trim were so much smoother, so much more polished than the old magnetic mountain of the *Thousand and One Nights*.

I thought back to the young businessman I had met during my first days in Cairo. I had called him the Doubter because of his rejection of martyrdom and everything it implied. The intolerance of the past, the fateful choice between conversion or death, the smell of blood, violence, proud zealotry, loyalty, truth, and tears – it all sounded strange and unlikely in this shopping mall where no such articles could be bought. And because absolutely everything else imaginable actually was in stock, there was no room for one to feel like something was missing. Wasn't this the solution to all those unsolvable issues, all the baggage that history sought to drag along into the present and the future? And wasn't this world without martyrs so much nicer? Who could still want to see an individual's faith so relentlessly put to the test – wouldn't that displease even the most pious nowadays?

An agonizing thought crept up on me and wouldn't let me go, much as I wished it away: if all Egypt had been a shopping mall, the murderers would not have become murderers and the martyrs would not have become martyrs. Brutality is a symptom of backwardness, but might faith that makes no concessions be as well? In churches the faithful were shrouded in clouds of incense; in New Cairo shoppers were spritzed with clouds of Chanel No. 5. Couldn't I see how the women's faces relaxed, how their eyes lit up?

Youssef

21

The Minority and the Majority

THE OWNER OF THE DOWNTOWN CAIRO HOTEL where I spent a few nights was a cosmopolitan, elegant man. His old-fashioned hotel had been established under the British Protectorate, and he cared for it solely out of a sense of filial piety. He also pursued various other interests: as a member of one of the city's most notable Coptic families, and as a member of the church's lay council, he was familiar with his country's history. The hotel was nearly empty, and as he passed by one evening he had nothing else to do, so he sat down next to me at the bar.

"Tensions between Muslims and Copts? Oh, that's overrated. We've lived together for ages. We're all Egyptians, we're neighbors, we do business with each other, we go through everything that's happening to this country together. We accompany our Muslim friends to the cemetery just as they do for our dead. Anyway, as a hotel owner I can deal with absolutely anyone. If you ask educated, modern Muslims about their relationship with Copts, they'll tell you there isn't the tiniest bit of trouble. Now, if you ask suitably educated Copts the same thing, they might mention one little issue or another. But some people always find something to complain about."

He paused, and took another tack.

"Take it from me, a solution to the Copts' problems is as hard to see today as it was a thousand years ago."

He spoke with a smile, as if there were no reason to worry.

"There's nothing special about our destiny. There isn't a country in the whole world where a minority could successfully coexist with a majority in any permanent way. We've been a minority for 1,400 years now, so we have a certain overview of the situation. And in our case, virtually everything makes it difficult or impossible to strike a balance."

He pronounced the word "impossible" almost triumphantly, while slapping his newspaper with the back of his hand. We had started out chatting about an article on peace talks in Syria, Israel, and the Gulf, but our conversation had quickly veered off toward the Copts.

"You have to imagine how all this started: the majority and minority are, first of all, two different peoples. The Arabs came from the desert and invaded us. I sometimes compare our fate with that of the Native Americans – the indigenous peoples who were plundered, decimated, deprived of their language, and marginalized by the English and Spanish conquistadors. But that's not all: many Native Americans who managed to survive became Christians, albeit not entirely voluntarily. There were and are conversions to Islam here, as well, but they only heighten the contrast, because we perceive it as a betrayal, a threat. Christians are forbidden to marry Muslims, because the children of such a marriage must always be Muslim. So there is no intermingling between the invaders and us, the natives who have become a minority. Our opposition is perpetually kept fresh."

He did not seem to regret this in the least; on the contrary, it sounded as if he were filled with pride by his people's persistent refusal to settle in with the Arab majority.

"So, next problem: the majority suspects the minority isn't loyal to the state, and somewhat dubiously sees it as yet another enemy. The fact that we were expelled from the Latin and Greek churches and fought alongside the Arabs to defeat the Crusaders doesn't help us Copts – we're Christians, and therefore seen as potential enemies of the Islamic majority which, in turn, has done and is doing everything to make it as difficult as possible for the Coptic minority to remain loyal. It's true that under the British Protectorate the English relied chiefly on the Copts to support their rule. My family did quite well back then. Among the English we were able to come up for air again, but we paid for it later on, when the republic abolished equal rights. Today, we're considered a fifth column – subversives in favor of the Americans."

His smile became less certain – perhaps because he thought this suspicion was not entirely unjustified.

I wanted to gently try to clarify what he was getting at: "Well, if that were the case, it wouldn't be entirely incomprehensible . . ."

He dismissed it: "Oh, c'mon. The Americans have done nothing but wreak havoc here."

Then he got us back on track.

"On to the next problem: the minority has been economically successful and thereby gained an influence that, in the eyes of the majority, exceeds what we're entitled to in terms of our share of the total population. As a German, you are surely aware of how that can turn out. 'The rich Copt' who sucks the poor folk dry, the parasite, the international mastermind who pulls all the right strings – that's a popular cliché in this country. And yet legislation has been passed to curtail our alleged influence: Copts can't hold leadership positions in national government, the military, or other administrative roles – the majority can't bear the idea that a Muslim would have to obey orders given by a Christian. But that only fuels the suspicion that Copts have secret, sinister ways of exerting their influence. It's a vicious cycle. And then comes yet another Egyptian specialty to settle the score: statistics. To this day, the Egyptian government refuses to figure out how many Copts there really are. Instead they just estimate, and spread the word that we make up only 8 to 10 percent of the population . . ."

I chimed in: "That's what every German newspaper says too."

He let out a hearty, derisive laugh. "We know we make up at least 20 percent of the Egyptian population – there are more of us than all Scandinavians combined. Of course, the smarter members of the Muslim Brotherhood have realized that such numbers would prevent their dream of an Islamic state from ever becoming a reality. But it was precisely the Muslim Brotherhood who fought so hard against President Mubarak's despotic regime – for democracy. And there's yet another problem: the Copts have little hope for democracy, and nothing to gain from it. This was immediately apparent after the Muslim Brotherhood's democratic victory. We are perpetually condemned to make some sort of arrangement with the despot of the day; and even then we don't exactly do well, though far better than when the majority party rules democratically. Our young intellectuals, including my own sons, were outraged when our pope tried to forbid them taking part in the demonstrations in Tahir Square, and they were even angrier when that same pope publicly sided with the new dictator. You still don't understand – do you? – that the concept of a secular state comes from the West and from Christianity; it has no roots here. The danger of making arrangements with despots is that they are always overthrown at some point, and then you are back on the wrong side of things; you are held responsible for all the corruption, violence, and incompetence. It is so unfortunate that the current president-general has failed to stop Copts from being slaughtered, and hasn't been able to restore public safety. It's a bad sign. If things keep up like this, soon I will have to close my hotel."

He lost himself in thought. I looked at him – there was so much more to say, but he wanted to change the subject.

"What conclusion do you draw from all this? What can be learned from it?"

My question stemmed from a hope that such a laid-back man with such a solid grasp on the bigger picture would have some practical solution at hand, or might know of some viable way out of this vexing situation.

"What can be learned from it?"

He instantly regained the good humor befitting a professional hotel owner.

"What can be learned from it? Whatever you do, don't belong to a minority! That's what can be learned!"

Epilogue: An Invisible Army

EVEN AS THE DIOCLETIANIC PERSECUTION raged on, a group of particularly determined Christians had begun coming together in Egypt to seek martyrdom. The patriarch of Alexandria condemned their willingness to suffer and claimed it only increased the intensity with which the faithful were being exterminated. This sparked a major debate that ultimately led to a schism, and the breakaway church called itself the "Church of the Martyrs."

But once the persecution had ended and the schism was finally resolved, the Coptic Church as a whole realized that this title was an apt description of itself. Their interpretation went so far as to refuse the new calendar followed by the Latin and Greek churches, who in the sixth century chose to measure time beginning from the birth of Christ; instead, the Copts continued to measure time beginning from Diocletian's accession to the imperial throne. The so-called *anno diocletiani,* or Diocletian era, had applied throughout the empire, but now became a core part of Copts' self-image. Thus, for them, the year 284 after Christ became 1 *anno martyrum,* or "Year 1 in the Era of the Martyrs," and this calendar remains in use today.

"We are the Church of Martyrs" is a phrase heard over and over in conversation with young Copts. It is the honorary title of the Coptic Church, but has also been undeniably prophetic. For throughout history, the Copts have been given countless opportunities to maintain their status as just that: a fellowship of martyrs. The period of Egypt's political exploitation as a Roman and, later, Eastern Roman province was an era of relative freedom for the Coptic Church, in which it had a decisive influence on the development of the Catholic and Orthodox faiths. One must admit that the Egyptians made the most of this brief period of communion with Rome and Byzantium not only by granting the church victory over Arianism at the First Council of Nicaea, but also by confirming the church's devotion to Mary as Mother of God at the Council of Ephesus and, through the legacy of Saint Anthony of Egypt, establishing the monastic tradition.

But the oppression of the Copts began early on, even as Alexandria and Constantinople were still deep in their own power struggle, and the Copts' earliest oppressors were fellow Christians. In 619, however, the Sassanid Persians conquered the land. They had already destroyed Jerusalem and the Church of the Holy Sepulcher, and now proceeded to reduce five hundred Coptic monasteries to rubble. The year 642 brought the Arab conquest, led by Caliph Umar. For the church, this marked the beginning of an almost interminable period of discrimination, humiliation, and impoverishment. A special tax was imposed on Christians, leading many to abandon their faith. They were excluded from the splendor of Islamic culture under the successive Fatimid Caliphate, Saladin's rule as vizier, and, later, the Mamluk Sultanate. Again and again, churches were burned to the ground, and none could be rebuilt. Copts were required to be outwardly recognizable by their dress. At times, they were forced to carry a five-pound cross around their necks.

Such relentless harassment and restrictions caused the Church of Martyrs to shrink. Cut off from the Latin

and Greek churches, more and more Copts gave up hope
and became Muslims, and the once primarily Christian
country became predominantly Islamic, with only a small
Coptic minority. By the sixteenth century, there were
only 112 churches left in a land that had once contained
thousands. The church lost its intellectual power. The
monasteries' precious libraries, most notably that of the
White Monastery in Sohag, were raided and dispersed;
today the Copts' written records are scattered from London
to Vienna, Naples, and a hundred other foreign cities. The
church was in such financial straits that it began selling
ecclesiastical offices, and at one point even the title of
bishop could be bought. The clergy were no longer educated,
there were now illiterate priests, and in remote areas years
passed without a priest being seen. Many Copts remained
unbaptized. The pressure of the Muslim environment led
some Copts to adopt Muslim customs, and here and there
polygamous Coptic families could be found. For a long time
the church even allowed divorce, despite Jesus' explicit ban,
and the license to divorce was only repealed in the 1950s,
with a great deal of effort.

The end seemed inevitable. The once-proud Church of
Martyrs, small and poor as it had become, was dealt one
humiliation after another, although even in those centuries its faithful repeatedly made great sacrifices for their
belief. Nevertheless, it seemed the laws of politics, history,
and sociology had condemned the church to die a slow,
inglorious death. Of course, under the Turks even Islamic
Egypt experienced the decline to which more or less all
lands subjected to Turkish rule were historically doomed,
whether in Europe or in the Near East. The somewhat
pretentious term for this process, *fellahization*, might no
longer be deployed so pompously, given the self-doubt that
has since befallen Western civilization. In any case, by this

time it was clear that the Copts were no longer alone in their state of atrophy: the entirety of Egypt had fallen into poverty and backwardness.

This, in a nutshell, is how Coptic historians described the history of the Egyptian church for me. They all regretted how little research was done within the church itself. Outside the ecclesiastical seminaries no chair for Coptology is permitted at any publicly-funded university, which is yet another example of the entrenched ignorance with which the majority looks down on its country's own indigenous people.

But another question now engrossed me: Would more historical research yield a better explanation of what actually happened in the middle of the nineteenth century, when, after more than a thousand years of decline, something in the Coptic Church started to stir again? The circumstances of its rebirth can certainly be described, but that does not diminish the mystery of how such a faint spark could so quickly turn into a blazing fire.

Perhaps a good place to start is with the Albanian-born tobacco merchant Muhammad Ali who – first as Ottoman Pasha and later as the de facto independent khedive, or viceroy, of the Sublime Porte – introduced Egypt to Western civilization. The subsequent inauguration of the Suez Canal then entangled the country in a new dependence on a major foreign power, but this time it was the British, whose Catholic and Protestant missionaries poured into the country and were able to work unhindered. One serious legal inequality the Copts had long suffered under was repealed at that time; the government abolished the poll tax on Christians. Meanwhile, the Copts adopted the use of Sunday schools from the Protestant missionaries, and the faithful finally began receiving regular religious instruction. Theological seminaries were created to educate priests, especially in the Coptic script and language. Old, almost totally abandoned monasteries began to fill up again, and to this day they exert such a pull that they are hardly able to accommodate all the aspiring postulants. Two charismatic popes then led the church from Saint Mark's Coptic Orthodox Cathedral, one right after the other: Pope Cyril VI (1959–1971), who was deeply committed to ascetic monasticism and is now revered as a saint; and Pope Shenouda III (1971–2012). The latter's reign saw renewed conflict between the Copts, the Egyptian government, and the country's Muslim majority. Shenouda himself had a falling out with President Sadat, who had encouraged the growth of Islamism in government legislation; because of Shenouda's protest against the move to base Egyptian law on Sharia law, Sadat banished him to the desert monastery of Saint Pishoy for four years.

But these measures were leveled against a newly strengthened church, and only stoked its enthusiasm. The Copts knew they enjoyed the protection of Blessed Mary, Mother of God, and they knew it long before she appeared before large crowds in Cairo. Who would refute their reading of the church's resurrection as a manifestation of divine will?

Not surprisingly, this resurgence has been a source of distrust and resistance by Egyptian Muslims. Indeed, the last few decades have brought an incessant string of horrific attacks on Coptic Christians, even before the rash of violence accompanying the recent civil war. Coptic Christianity's reemergence coincides with the ongoing expulsion and murder of Christians in Iraq and Syria. Virtually everywhere else, the centuries-long coexistence of Muslims and Christians seems to have ended; Egypt is the sole holdout against the prevailing tendency toward religious homogenization in regions under Muslim rule.

But what is going on in Egypt does not exactly look like real peace between the religions, and the Pope of

Alexandria and his bishops have repeatedly implored their people to exercise the utmost caution in this precarious situation. In fact, they usually remain silent about attacks on Copts, and even remind the faithful of Jesus' instruction to turn the other cheek – not just spiritually, but quite literally, in hopes of defusing the country's explosive mood – an attitude many Coptic intellectuals criticize.

Meanwhile, simply by renouncing revenge and retribution, the invisible army of martyrs grows, ever greater and ever more powerful.

Acknowledgments

The author would like to thank everyone who granted him access to the Coptic world: the parents and relatives of the Twenty-One, for their warm welcome to El-Aour and the images they generously provided; H. E. Bishop Anba Damian, Bishop of the Copts in Germany, for the connections in Egypt; H. Em. Metropolitan Anba Pavnutios of Samalut and H. Ex. Bishop Anba Thomas of Assiut for their generous support in Samalut; Prince Asfa-Wossen Asserate of Ethiopia, for a preliminary introduction to the particuliarities of the Coptic Church; Abuna Bolla and Abuna Timotheus, as well as the nuns of the El Mohareb Monastery, for their gracious hospitality; Mina Farag and Ibrahim Saad Ibrahim for their patient assistance in El-Aour; Prof. Georges Khalil and Prof. Magued Girgis for their invaluable advice; Dr. Alfred Huber and Mohammed Ameen for their inspired tour of Cairo; Paul Badde, who – as editor of *Vatican* magazine – placed the photo of St. Kiryollos's head on the cover.

I am indebted to the book *Geschichte und Geist der koptischen Kirche* ("The History and Spirit of the Coptic Church"), edited by Wolfgang Boochs (Aachen: Bernardus-Verlag, 2009), for numerous references, suggestions, and general information.